IMAGES
of America

EAGLE RIVER

IMAGES
of America

EAGLE RIVER

Zane Treesh

ARCADIA
PUBLISHING

Published by Arcadia Publishing
Charleston, South Carolina

Library of Congress Control Number: 2013938247

For all general information, please contact Arcadia Publishing:
Telephone 843-853-2070
Fax 843-853-0044
E-mail sales@arcadiapublishing.com
For customer service and orders:
Toll-Free 1-888-313-2665

Visit us on the Internet at www.arcadiapublishing.com

To my wife, Robin, and our daughters, Rebecca Rose and Anna Ruth

CONTENTS

ACKNOWLEDGMENTS

I would like to thank Phyllis Smith and Nanette Belk of the Chugiak–Eagle River Historical Society for letting me use photographs from the society's collection, for taking the time to talk about the history of Eagle River, and for helping search through the collection to find images. A thank-you goes to Suzi Groski with the Chugiak–Eagle River Chamber of Commerce for letting me use images from its collection, especially the ones regarding the Bear Paw Festival. The VFW Post No. 9785, Iditarod Checkpoint No. 1, was very supportive and let me go through the photo albums they have compiled.

Helen Phillips deserves special mention for sharing her photographs and the stories that go with them. She was very helpful. Her pictures show what Eagle River was like in the 1950s, 1960s, and 1970s.

A thank-you goes to my parents, Jim and Linda Treesh, for making the decision to move to Eagle River in 1971 and providing a wonderful environment in which to grow up. Gratitude also goes to my mom for reading through my manuscript with an editor's eye.

I must mention Archie Boyles. He was a wonderful man and longtime friend who moved to Alaska in the early 1950s and stayed for the rest of his life. Archie lived in Eagle River for most of those years. He was a relative of my wife, and Robin and I met when she came up to visit him. When Archie passed away in 2009, he left his photograph collection to us, and without it, this book would not have been possible.

I could not have written this book without the support of my wife, Robin. She put up with me as I took the time to write and then as we edited the material together.

I want to thank my Lord and Savior, Jesus Christ, for providing the resources and time to do this book.

INTRODUCTION

According to Shem Pete in *Shem Pete's Alaska*, the Dena'ina Indians used Eagle River valley for hunting and fishing long before nonnative explorers visited the area. During the 1890s, gold was discovered in the creeks along Turnagain Arm. Almost certainly, prospectors visited the valley at this time; however, they did not leave any records of their travels. The first written account of traveling in the Eagle River area is Walter C. Mendenhall's report "A Reconnaissance From Resurrection Bay to the Tanana River, Alaska, in 1898." Part of his paper describes the group's travels through Eagle River valley. Just a few years after Mendenhall's trip, a trail was made for passage of people and supplies to different mining camps between Seward, in the south, and Nome, in the north. When gold was discovered in 1908, and the town of Iditarod was formed; the name Iditarod was also given to the trail.

The construction of the Alaska Railroad began in 1915. The railroad was built to connect the large interior mining district around Fairbanks with the sea at Seward. Anchorage began at the mouth of Ship Creek as the headquarters for the Alaska Engineering Commission, which had the task of building the railroad. About 10 miles north of Anchorage, the railroad had to cross Eagle River, and a large bridge was built. Soon, a road also ran in that direction and was, for a while, called the Eagle River Road.

In 1930, a congressional grant was given to Siebenthaler to be used for a fur farm around Lower Fire Lake. This was an extension of the fur farming that had been going on around Anchorage. The grant around Lower Fire Lake, between Eagle River and the Knik River, was the first land that was not claimed by the government. Slowly, families started moving into this area in the mid-1930s to mid-1940s. In 1943, Glenn Briggs first saw the Eagle River area. That year, he purchased a homestead from Jack Cobel and set up a hog operation to sell meat to nearby Fort Richardson. Glenn convinced his brother Dale to homestead the land next to his in 1945.

World War II had brought lots of people to Alaska and opened up possibilities in the Anchorage and Eagle River areas. Several families homesteaded in the vicinity of Eagle River in the late 1940s and early 1950s. In 1947, Walter Pippel purchased the homestead of Lars Nyberg. Pippel farmed the large field that was part of this land. The field contained fertile soil, and Walter grew a variety of vegetable crops to sell. The Pippel name became engrained in the history of Eagle River because of the family's yellow house and the large field they farmed. Even after it was populated with homes and businesses, this field has continued to be known as Pippel's Field.

Homesteaders, including Art and Eleanor Braendel, Raymond and Lucille Tedrow, Tony Brockstahler, and Jack and Phyllis Stewart, played prominent roles in Eagle River's development. They left lasting impressions on the area.

In 1955, Vern and Helen Phillips started running a small trailer court for Dale Briggs on part of his property that fronted the Glenn Highway. Helen took pictures during her three years of living at this location. When the Army transferred Vern to Arizona, they both had hopes of moving back to Eagle River. When they did return, they bought the Texaco station in the middle of Eagle River, located next to the Glenn Highway, in 1965. Vern and Helen ran the business for the next 10 years; during that time, Helen continued to record the changes to Eagle River with photographs.

The Eagle River Shopping Center was opened in 1956 through the efforts of Glenn Briggs, Raymond Tedrow, and Evelyn Sehm. It was a modern building, with the area's first full-service grocery store, the Market Basket, which had a meat counter. Several churches were started during this time period, including the First Baptist Church of Eagle River.

Eagle River Elementary School was opened in 1960, and the students no longer had to go to Chugiak. Four years later, Chugiak High School opened halfway between Eagle River and Chugiak, and the high school students no longer had to ride the bus to Anchorage.

The Eagle River Shopping Center was expanded in 1960 and again in 1965. The Greater Anchorage Area Borough was formed in 1963. It was created to serve as the political equivalent of a county in the Lower 48. Glenn Briggs was the first assemblyman to represent the Eagle River area.

The Good Friday earthquake of 1964 shook the area hard for almost four minutes. Minor damage was reported in Eagle River. One of the more costly types of damage in the area was the blockage of the flow of water into some families' wells due to the ground having shifted.

Toward the end of the 1960s, the Glenn Highway was rerouted around downtown Eagle River. Businesses feared the loss of customers, but the growth in the area more than made up for less business from highway travelers.

In the 1970s, the construction of the Trans-Alaska Pipeline took place from 1974 to 1977. Although its was not near the construction sites for the pipeline, a number of workers and their families moved into the area, and new subdivisions were built. One could look up during this time period and frequently see gray C-130s with orange tails, which were carrying people and supplies to the work sites.

In the 1980s, as money poured into the state of Alaska from the oil production royalties, the population of Eagle River exploded. In 1973, a developer had purchased 90 acres of Pippel's Field. By the early 1980s, development of the property began in earnest. Business Boulevard was built, and businesses were constructed along it. In the years 1984 and 1985, the following projects were completed: Valley River Office Center, the Regional Park Plaza, the Valley River Cinemas, Eagle River Bowling Alley, and the Valley River Complex. The Briggs Bridge was opened in 1992, allowing Eagle River Loop Road to be connected with Hiland Road and the Glenn Highway.

Two annual gatherings were well established by this time period. The Highland Games have been held at Lions Park in early August since 1981, and the Chugiak–Eagle River Chamber of Commerce started the Bear Paw Festival in 1986, which continue today. As the years have passed, both have grown larger, and Eagle River's history continues to be written.

One

EARLY EXPLORATION, IDITAROD TRAIL, AND ALASKA RAILROAD
1898–1930

Before 1898, there was nothing recorded regarding the exploration of Eagle River valley. Alaska Natives and prospectors had traveled up and down the length of the valley but did not write about those early journeys. When the Klondike goldfield in the Yukon Territory was discovered in 1896, the public and the US government wanted as much information as they could get on the territory of Alaska. In 1898, Walter C. Mendenhall, a US Geological Survey geologist, accompanied Military Expedition No. 3, which was led by Capt. Edwin F. Glenn of the 25th Infantry, US Army. They traveled from Turnagain Arm to the Tanana River and back. Walter C. Mendenhall's account, first published in the *20th Annual Report of the United States Geological Survey*, describes their travels over Crow Pass and down Eagle River valley. Based on the local name for it, the river was called Yukla Creek by W.C. Mendenhall. By 1904, in *United States Geological Survey Bulletin No. 277*, "Mineral Resources of the Kenai Peninsula, Alaska," the river is referred to as "Eagle, or Yukla, Creek."

The route that Mendenhall's group had taken in 1898 became a part of the original route of the Iditarod Trail from Seward to Nome. The trail took its name from the prominent mining district and town of Iditarod, where gold was discovered in 1908. That was the same year that improvements were made to the trail so that supplies could be taken to the mining districts and gold could be hauled to the coast to be shipped. The Eagle River valley saw heavy traffic, especially in the winter, until the completion of the Alaska Railroad in 1923.

The 1916 *Annual Report of the Alaska Engineering Commission for the Alaska Railroad* contains a 1912 map of the area around Anchorage. The map lists the river as Yukla Creek. However, by that time, the locals were already referring to it as the Eagle River, and the name Yukla Creek was quickly fading. Eagle River was the first large river that had to be crossed by the railroad north of Anchorage. In November 1915, work was started on the bridge. A small group of politicians and prominent Alaskans went to the construction site for a photo shoot with one of the railroad's official photographers. Sydney Laurence took pictures of the group holding a sign proclaiming the Anchorage-to-Fairbanks Special. Among the men shown in front of the incomplete bridge are Judge Wickersham and "Cap" Lathrop.

Walter C. Mendenhall's report "A Reconnaissance from Resurrection Bay to the Tanana River, Alaska, in 1898," in the *20th Annual Report of the United States Geological Survey* contains this map section. The report was the first written account of exploration of the Eagle River valley. At the time, it was called Yukla Creek, as shown on this map. (*20th Annual Report of the United States Geological Survey, 1898–1899.*)

This photograph was taken from the area where Raven Valley connects with Eagle River valley, and was probably the first view of Eagle Glacier seen by Walter Mendenhall's party. In the summer of 1898, Eagle Glacier would have been a little farther down the valley. Just a few years later, a roadhouse serving the trail was built near this site. (Author's collection.)

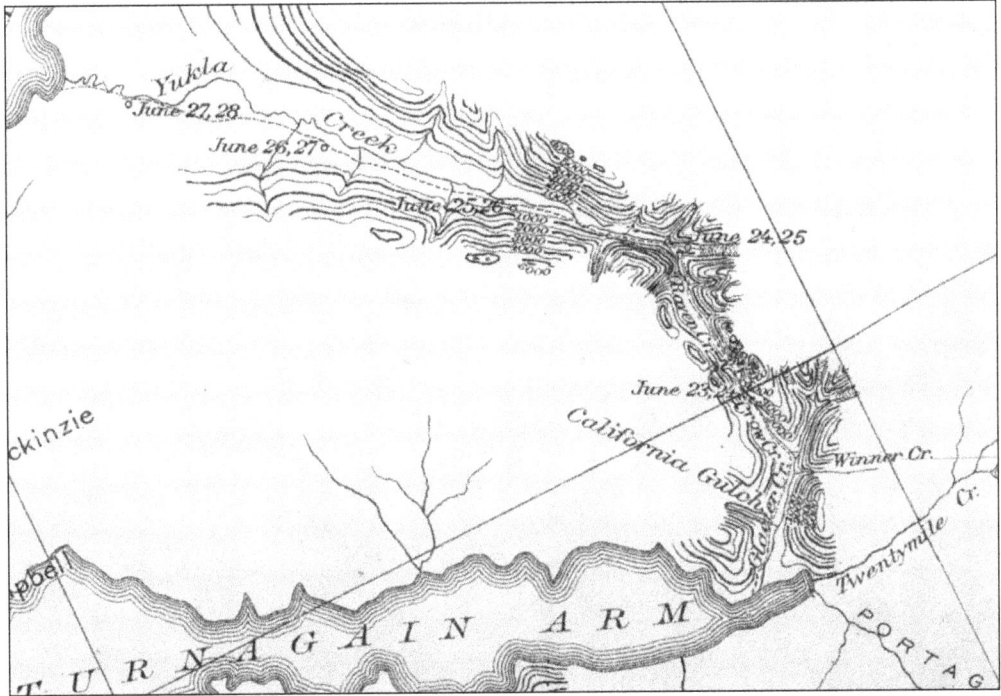

A close-up of the map published with Walter C. Mendenhall's report shows Eagle River as Yukla Creek. The location and dates of each campsite the group made in the valley can be seen as well. The mosquitoes were so horrendous they had to set up their first camp on a gravel bar to avoid the massive swarms. (*20th Annual Report of the United States Geological Survey, 1898–1899.*)

Around 1908, the Burchett family traveled through Eagle River valley on the original Iditarod Trail, going to the new mining town of Iditarod. It must have been a fairly rough trail for on the back of this photograph is written "Roadhouse at Eagle River. We had to stop here a half day to repair our sled which was badly broken." The old Eagle River roadhouse was located near the mouth of Meadow Creek. During this time period, roadhouses were usually located about 20 miles apart along the trail. (Burchett Collection, Anchorage Museum, B1991.25.002.)

The group is getting ready to visit the construction site of the railroad bridge over Eagle River in November 1915. Judge James Wickersham (third from right) was at this time a delegate to Congress from the Territory of Alaska. Austin "Cap" Lathrop (far right) was an entrepreneur who has been described as Alaska's first homegrown millionaire. (Sydney Laurence, Alaska State Archives, P277.006.063.)

Looking north, this image shows construction of the railroad bridge over Eagle River on November 12, 1915. For scale, one can see an individual to the left of the framework. Work on the railroad did not slow down during the winter months. (Sydney Laurence, Alaska State Archives, P277.006.007.)

At the site of the Eagle River railroad bridge, a group standing on a flatbed railroad car holds up a sign proclaiming the Anchorage-to-Fairbanks Special. Judge Wickersham is fourth from the right. In 1916, he would introduce the first Alaska Statehood Bill. It would be over 40 years before Alaska became a state. Standing a little lower to the left, by himself, is Cap Lathrop. (Sydney Laurence, Alaska State Archives, P277.006.066.)

A little over three months later, on February 28, 1916, this picture shows a train about to cross Eagle River. On this trip, the railroad was only completed to about Knik River, so the train is probably taking supplies to the end of the line for construction. (Sydney Laurence, Alaska State Archives, P277.006.009.)

Not long after the completion of the railroad bridge over Eagle River, Sydney Laurence took this photograph on February 28, 1916. During the first couple years of railroad construction, Laurence was one of the official photographers for the Alaska Engineering Commission. He had a photograph shop in Anchorage during this time period; however, he earned his fame as one of Alaska's greatest painters. Laurence is known for his majestic paintings of Alaska, especially those depicting Mount McKinley. (Sydney Laurence, Alaska Railroad Collection, Anchorage Museum, B1979.002.L49.)

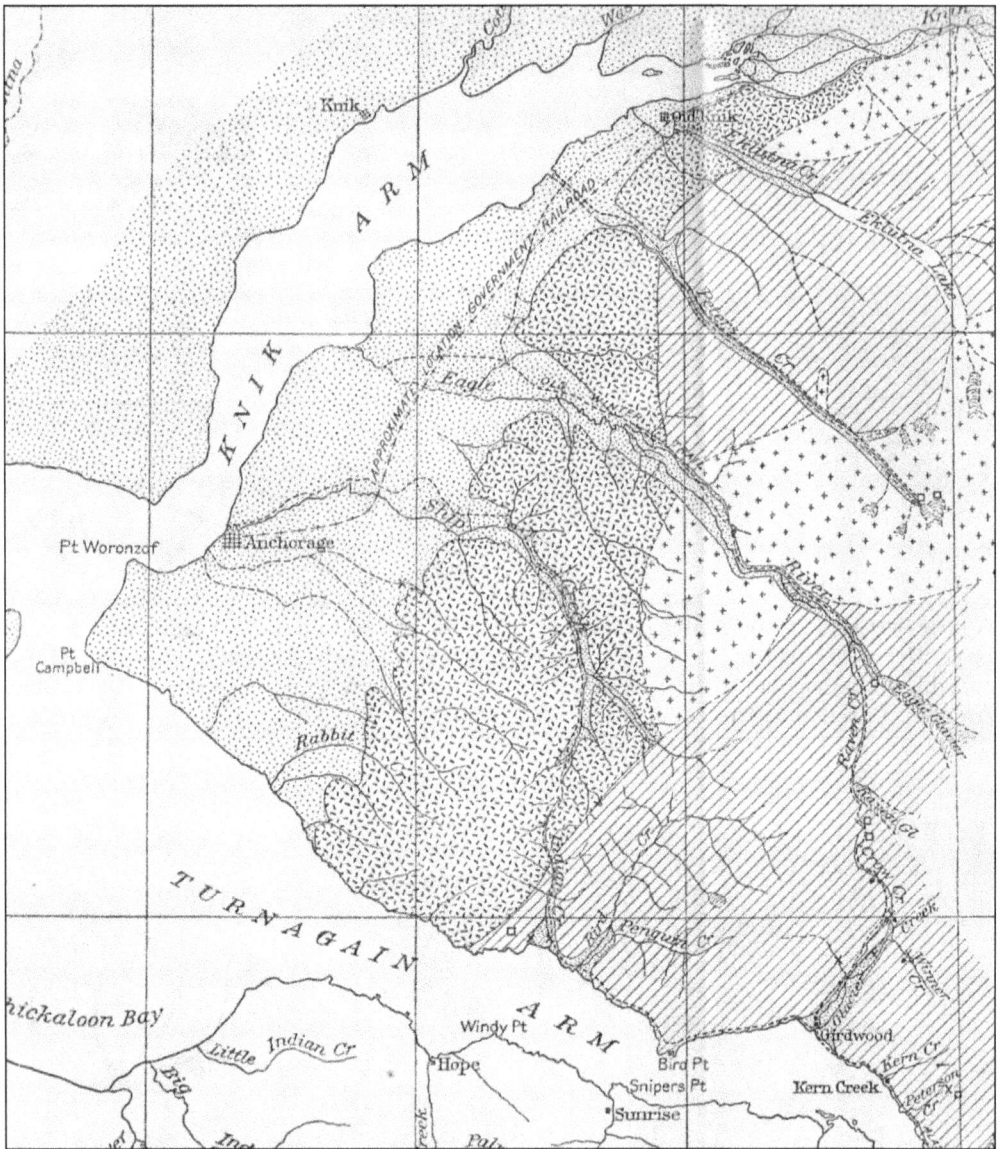

A map from *US Geological Survey Bulletin No. 642* shows the area between Knik and Turnagain Arms in 1916. The Alaska Railroad has only reached the Knik River, and the Iditarod Trail can be seen as the old trail going up Eagle River valley and over to Girdwood. The new town of Anchorage is shown near the mouth of Ship Creek. (*United States Geological Survey Bulletin No. 642, 1916.*)

This picture was taken during World War I, in 1917 or 1918. It shows a soldier standing on the Eagle River Bridge, wearing mosquito netting. World War I took a lot of the resources away from the building of the Alaska Railroad. It would not be completed for another five years, in 1923. (Alaska Railroad Collection, Anchorage Museum, B1979.002.H56.)

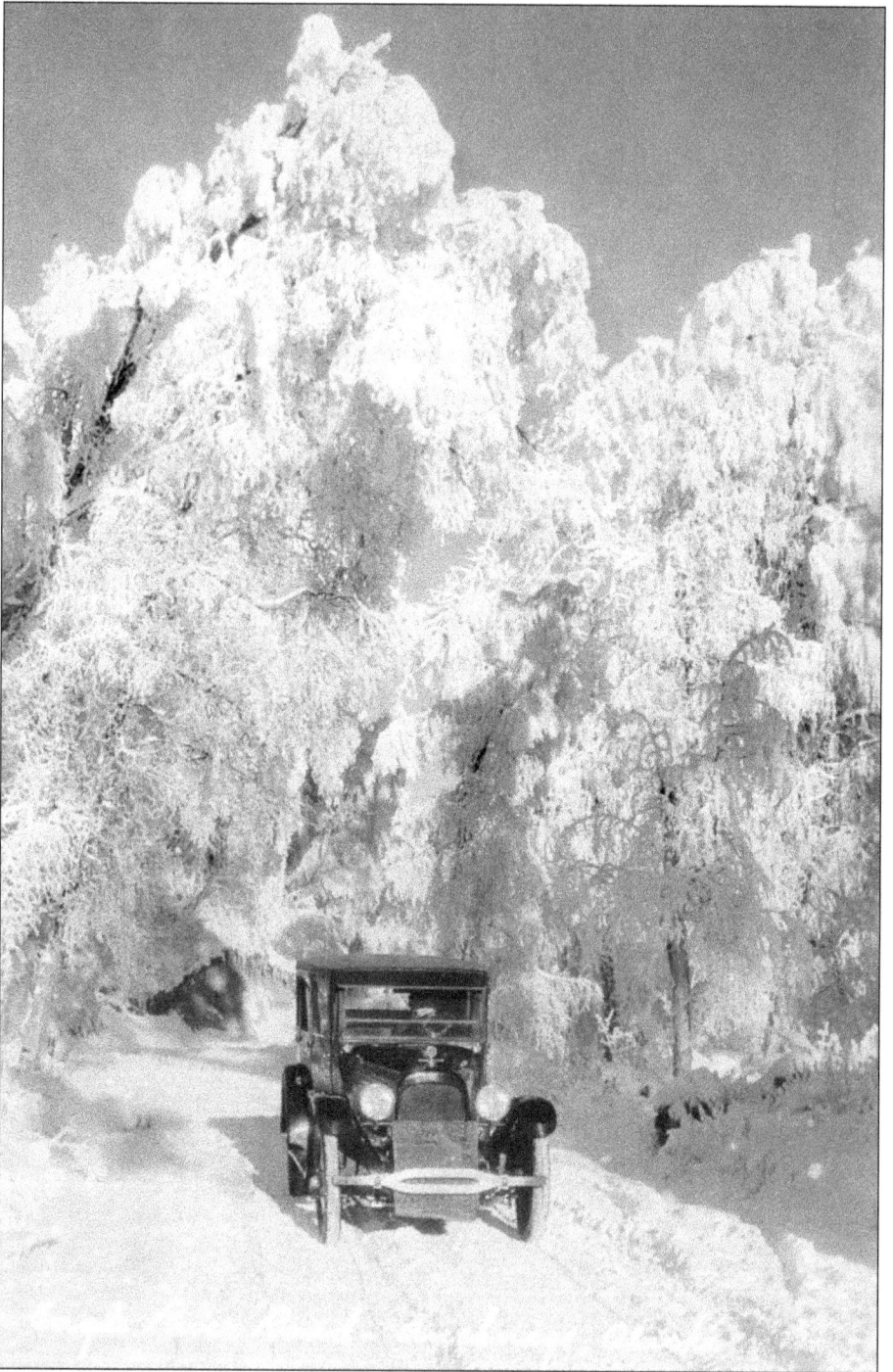

This postcard shows a winter scene from the 1920s of a car on the Eagle River Road, which ran north from Anchorage. The *Cordova Daily Times: All Alaska Section Review for 1927* shows a photograph of the road and already refers to it as "the Eagle River Road." During World War II, the Glenn Highway was built on this route to connect Anchorage to the new Alaska Highway. (Holiday Collection, Anchorage Museum, B1981.031.03.)

Two

First Homesteaders and Settlers
1930–1950

In 1930, the first private property between Eagle River and Knik River was a congressional grant given to Siebenthaler for 300-plus acres. The land included all of Lower Fire Lake and the area adjacent to it. The grant was given for a fur farm. In 1935, Ken Laughlin filed on 160 acres taking in all of Upper Fire Lake. The cabin Ken built in the summer of 1935 was the first residence in the area. During that summer, he set up a stand in front of his cabin to sell hot dogs to construction crews working on the highway running to Palmer. This was the first merchandizing venture in the Eagle River area.

Lars Nyberg became Ken Laughlin's first neighbor when Lars homesteaded in 1937. This area later became part of Pippel's Field. According to some accounts, the Nybergs bought their house through Sears, Roebuck & Co. Walter Pippel purchased the Nybergs' homestead in 1947. His house would become known as the yellow Pippel house for the next several decades. Glenn Briggs came to Eagle River in 1943 and decided it would be a good area in which to raise pigs. His business, the Anchorage Livestock Co., purchased Jack Cobel's 150-acre homestead in 1943. Glenn told his brother Dale about the area, and in 1945, Dale and his wife, Ruth, homesteaded 160 acres adjacent to Glenn and Mary Lou. Both Briggs couples stayed on their homesteads for the remainder of their lives.

The late 1940s brought other families to the area who would make important contributions to the community. In 1947, Art and Eleanor Braendel homesteaded 160 acres on Meadow Creek, uphill from the Briggs property. That same year, Raymond and Lucille Tedrow claimed 160 acres next to the big hill of what was later called Eagle River Loop Road.

Glenn and Mary Briggs pose at the Cobol homestead they purchased in 1943. The small dog at Mary's feet is a Pomeranian. Mary was fond of this breed of dogs. In the 1990s, she could still be seen walking her Pomeranians along the Old Glenn Highway near her house. (Chugiak–Eagle River Historical Society.)

This was the first house the Briggses lived in on their property. It was a cabin with a flat roof near Meadow Creek. Mount Baldy can be seen on the horizon behind the house. The moose rack over the garage was a standard decoration for early settlers. (Chugiak–Eagle River Historical Society.)

The Briggs family had moved to the area to raise pigs. They set up pigpens next to Meadow Creek. In 1950, the Vanovers bought the pig operation and 40 acres from the Briggses. Eventually, the area became Vanover Drive off Old Eagle River Road. (Chugiak–Eagle River Historical Society.)

Needing a place to care for the pigs indoors, especially during the cold winters, the Briggses built this shed for farrows shortly after purchasing the property in 1943. This photograph shows the shed in 1944. (Chugiak–Eagle River Historical Society.)

This is how Glenn and Mary Briggs' cabin looked in 1944. After Glenn sold his pig operation, he began building up Eagle River. He established a water utility in the area and developed and marketed one of Eagle River's first subdivisions. (Chugiak–Eagle River Historical Society.)

Dale and Ruth Briggs homesteaded 160 acres next to his brother Glenn's property in 1945. This shows the first house they built. During the 1950s, they had a small trailer park on their property. Vern and Helen Phillips managed it from 1955 to 1958. (Chugiak–Eagle River Historical Society.)

In this late-1940s image, potatoes are being harvested on Walter Pippel's homestead. Students from the Eklutna Industrial School usually helped with the harvest. (Chugiak–Eagle River Historical Society.)

Walter Pippel holds a couple of potatoes from his field in 1947. Walter said he averaged at least 12–14 tons of potatoes per acre. The family also raised cabbage and other vegetables to sell. He used to have a large barn near the Texaco station on the Glenn Highway. It was lost to fire near the end of the 1960s. (Chugiak–Eagle River Historical Society.)

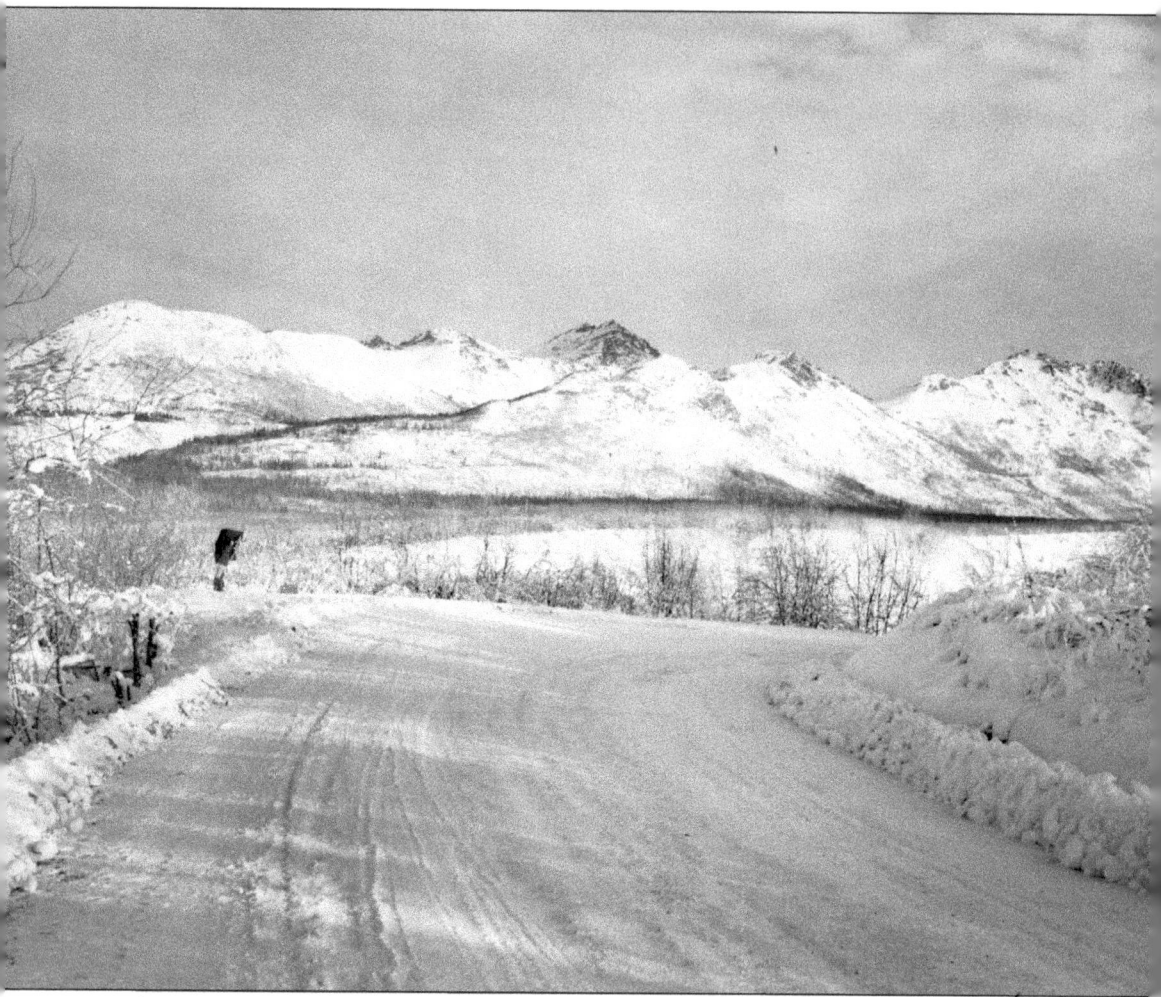

A winter shot taken in the 1940s from the top of the hill leading down to the bridge over Eagle River shows Mount Baldy and part of the Chugach Mountains on the north side of the valley. Drivers dreaded this part of the trip going north out of Anchorage. At the bottom of the hill, the road made a sharp turn to the left to cross the river. When icy, it was very dangerous. (Sidney Hamilton Photograph Collection, Anchorage Museum, B1976.082.165.)

Three

Beginning of Commercial Buildings
1950–1960

A number of families moved into the area during the 1950s. Jack and Phyllis Stewart homesteaded their 160 acres in 1952 about 3.5 miles back Eagle River valley along what would become Eagle River Road. There were eight families in the area east of what would become the Eagle River Loop Road. One of the Donaho families proved up on its homestead while using a tent as the family home. Danny Bell and his wife, Shirley, homesteaded 160 acres in the area. The property eventually became the Eaglewood subdivision. Over the years, Danny purchased other homesteads adjacent to his. He subdivided one, drilled a well on it, and put in a water system. According to Danny, the well could provide enough water to support 10,000 people. He named the streets in this subdivision after famous racehorses.

In 1950, Matanuska Electric Association ran a power line from Eklutna to Fred Hahn's property, which was just past Danny Bell's. Matanuska Telephone Association brought telephones to the area for the first time in April 1957. When the phones went into service, there were 13 subscribers in the area.

To promote interest and raise money in Chugiak and Eagle River for various community needs, a spring carnival was started in 1954. The profits went to US Public Health Service Nursing, Little League, the fire company, parent-teacher association (PTA), and other organizations. The first carnival was held at a large gravel area near Dale Briggs's homestead. Eventually, the Eagle River Elementary School was built at this location. The first carnival was such a success that it became an annual event held over Memorial Day weekend. The location of the carnival was later moved to Chugiak and held for a number of years.

In 1955, Raymond Tedrow, Glenn Briggs, and Evelyn Sehm worked together to build the Eagle River Shopping Center. The shopping center opened in 1956 and became an anchor around which the businesses of Eagle River were built. When the shopping center opened, it was as modern as any in Alaska. The Market Basket grocery store occupied the north end. The post office opened here at the shopping center before moving to a new building on Coronado Road a few years later.

Tony Bockstahler proved up on a homestead in 1952. This photograph shows the wood shop on his property from which he ran a business. The homestead was located near Danny Bell's property along Eagle River Road. (Chugiak–Eagle River Historical Society.)

This view, taken from behind the Alaska Range Garage in 1953, looks across the Glenn Highway in the vicinity of Tips Bar and Santa Maria Drive. Mount Baldy can be seen in the upper middle of the photograph. (Chugiak–Eagle River Historical Society.)

A bird's-eye view shows the Eagle River Bridge in October 1953. In the 1960s, a new bridge was built at the same location. On the right side of the river, looking upstream, is where the Eagle River Campground is presently located. (Steve McCutcheon, Steve McCutcheon Collection, Anchorage Museum, B1990.014.5.TV.49.1.)

Far upstream from the main bridge, one can see the old bridge once used for crossing Eagle River. The road leading down to the bridge was later used to access the campground. When the Iditarod Trail Sled Dog Race ran to Eagle River, the dog teams crossed on the frozen river near the location of the Glenn Highway Bridge. (Steve McCutcheon, Steve McCutcheon Collection, Anchorage Museum, B1990.14.5.TV.49.2)

This is a view from a plane in October 1953 looking downstream over the Glenn Highway and bridge. Meadow Creek can be seen coming into the river from the right side next to the highway. Salmon are sometimes seen going up the creek during late summer. (Steve McCutcheon, Steve McCutcheon Collection, Anchorage Museum, B1990.14.5.TV.49.6.)

In 1954, the people of Eagle River held a big spring carnival on a large gravel lot across from Dale Briggs's homestead. The first carnival was pretty elaborate for the size of the community. There was a large stage for announcements and shows, and a number of booths were set up. Just for the carnival, Vern Haik was elected mayor of the community. This photograph shows him and his daughter Beverly at the carnival. (Chugiak–Eagle River Historical Society.)

During the spring carnival in 1954, this is one of the games of skill. After the first carnival in Eagle River, the event was moved to Chugiak. The second Chugiak Elementary School was later built at the Chugiak carnival location. (Chugiak–Eagle River Historical Society.)

At the first spring carnival in 1954, a motorcycle race was held. The carnival brought many people out from Anchorage to participate. It was so successful that the carnival became an annual event. (Chugiak–Eagle River Historical Society.)

This picture was taken of the motorcycle race during the first spring carnival in Eagle River in 1954. Six years later, in 1960, Eagle River Elementary School was built at this location. (Chugiak–Eagle River Historical Society.)

Vern Phillips is using a small dozer to do some work around the trailer court of Dale Briggs. It looks small but beats shoveling! Vern had hand-shoveled dirt from the Eagle River Shopping Center construction site and delivered it to residences needing fill dirt. (Helen Phillips family collection.)

Ward Wells took this shot of the exterior of the Market Basket on June 14, 1960. The Market Basket occupied the north end of the Eagle River Shopping Center. Wells was a professional photographer best known for his images of Anchorage from the 1940s to the 1980s. (Ward Wells, Ward Wells Collection, Anchorage Museum, B1983.91.C4327.)

This 1950s image shows the residence of Vern and Helen Phillips, who managed Dale Briggs's trailer court. Anchorage's population had grown so fast, due to World War II and the years after, that housing could not keep up with demand. It was not unusual for people in Eagle River and Anchorage to live in trailers and houses of this size. (Helen Phillips family collection.)

Here are Roy and Mary Vittitoe, friends of Vern and Helen Phillips, with the Phillipses' eldest daughter, Beverly, in 1956. Behind them is the area where First Baptist Church of Eagle River was eventually built. This was taken at the north end of the trailer park. There were few buildings around. (Helen Phillips family collection.)

Ray and Doreen Coates clean their car at the washroom in the middle of the small trailer park. In the 1950s, the washroom was where people washed their laundry inside and their cars outside. This was located across from where Eagle River Elementary School was built later. (Helen Phillips family collection.)

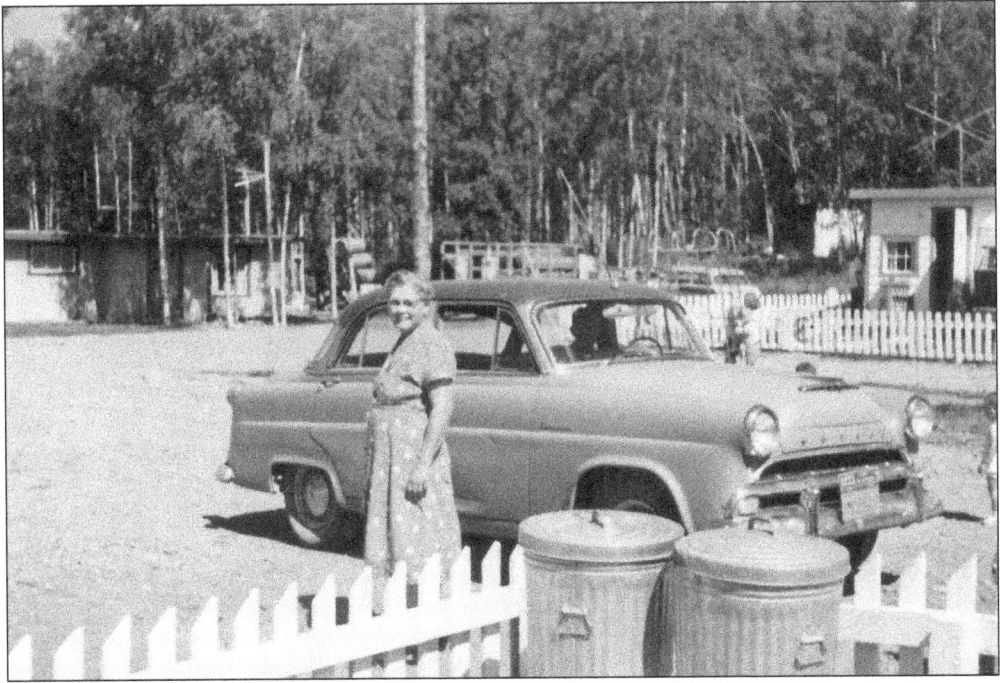

This picture, taken in the mid-1950s, shows the north end of a trailer court that used to be across from Eagle River Elementary School. Duplexes were built on the site of the old trailer court around 2005. (Helen Phillips family collection.)

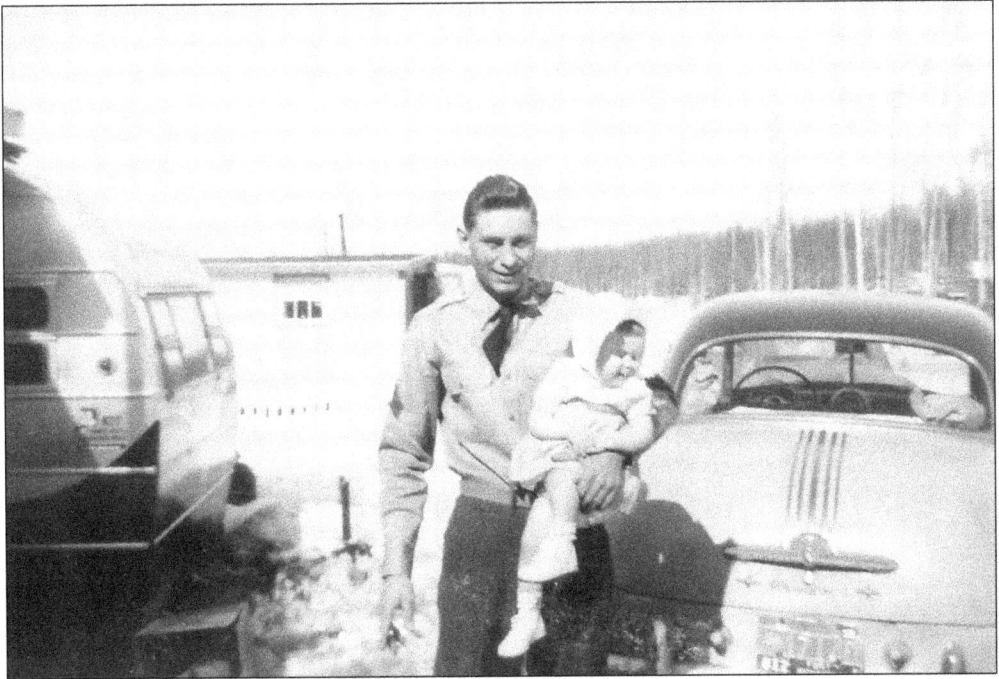

Vern Phillips and his daughter Beverly are ready for Easter Sunday in the mid-1950s at the trailer court he and his wife managed. (Helen Phillips family collection.)

Part of the interior of the First Baptist Church of Eagle River is shown in this photograph. During the 1950s and 1960s, many churches were started in the area. Over time, most of those earlier churches have built larger sanctuaries. (First Baptist Church of Eagle River.)

This group shot was taken in 1959 at Vacation Bible School held in the First Baptist Church of Eagle River. The building is located to the right of Monte Drive. A large parking lot to the left across the street was later cleared for the first Eagle River Bowl location. (First Baptist Church of Eagle River.)

Four

Downtown Development
1960–1970

In the 1960s, Eagle River was developed even more. The Eagle River Shopping Center was expanded in 1960 and again in 1965. In 1960, the Eagle River Elementary School was built, and students no longer had to ride a bus to Chugiak. The Eagle River Bowl with 10 lanes was built on Monte Drive just off of the Glenn Highway. Walter and Marion Bowen moved into the area in 1959. They cleared a lot, built, and began to operate the Lamp Post Inn and Restaurant in the early 1960s. It was located on the Glenn Highway directly across from the Texaco station.

In 1963, the Greater Anchorage Area Borough was formed following the guidelines of the Alaska Constitution. Boroughs set up throughout the state were equivalent to counties in the Lower 48.

After lobbying by citizens of the Chugiak and Eagle River areas, a high school was finally built. It was halfway between Eagle River and Chugiak and opened in 1964. The school was named Chugiak High after the committee flipped a coin to decide if it should be named for Eagle River or Chugiak. The high school students in the area no longer had to ride a bus to and from Anchorage.

On March 27, 1964, the Good Friday earthquake occurred, lasting around four minutes. The Market Basket aisles were filled with merchandise from the shelves, and other businesses suffered the same fate. A couple of the gym walls at the Eagle River Elementary School collapsed. No serious injuries were reported in the area.

The First Baptist Church of Eagle River constructed an addition in 1965, complete with a tall steeple and maroon siding. In the 1960s, other denominations built larger, or more permanent structures, including the St. Andrew Catholic Church. In 1965, the Eagle River Library opened. Three years later, Billie Moore, who had opened the Eagle River Library, and Polly Kallenberg, who had opened the Chugiak Library, merged the two into the Chugiak–Eagle River Library.

First Baptist Church of Eagle River met in this small building until the congregation constructed an addition in 1965. This image shows the new roof and siding in the early 1960s. The church building was still surrounded by woods. (First Baptist Church of Eagle River.)

In 1964, the Eagle River Shopping Center, which is located in the center of this photograph, had not been expanded to its present size. At the front of the building is the Glenn Highway, and Pippel's Field is not developed. Behind the shopping center are a few trailers. Only a couple of other buildings are in this part of town. (First Baptist Church of Eagle River.)

In this view looking upstream, this is the modern steel railroad bridge spanning Eagle River. A wooden structure was built in 1916, which was later replaced by a steel bridge. According to *The Alaska Earthquake March 27, 1964, Effects on Transportation and Utilities the Geological Survey Professional Paper 545-D*, this bridge was only slightly damaged by the quake. (Alaska Railroad Collection, Anchorage Museum, B1979.002.244.)

Since the 1950s, the communities of Chugiak and Eagle River had sent high school students to Anchorage by bus. Taken in December 1965, this photograph shows what Chugiak High looked like the second year after it opened. Over the years, the school has been added to and remodeled many times. (Chugiak–Eagle River Historical Society.)

During the 1960s, the bus picked the kids up in front of the Texaco station and the Lamp Post Inn. When Eagle River Elementary School was built in 1960, the bus route became a lot shorter for the students, who no longer had to travel to Chugiak for school. (Helen Phillips family collection.)

A man is filling his truck at the Texaco station along the Glenn Highway. Later, the Glenn Highway was routed around Eagle River. The name of the road in front of the station was changed to the Old Glenn Highway. This photograph was taken during the late 1960s. (Helen Phillips family collection.)

This image shows the Glenn Highway going south through town in the late 1960s. The Tastee Freez sign can be seen on the opposite side of the road just to the left of the gas pumps. Not many buildings had been built along the highway. (Helen Phillips family collection.)

A tractor is being used in Pippel's Field around late 1960s. A land speculator, Dick Rapp, bought Pippel's Field in 1973 when Eagle River was just beginning to really grow. Toward the end of the 1980s, the same individual, in an article in the *Anchorage Daily News*, said that buying the 90 acres of land was the best deal he had ever made. (Helen Phillips family collection.)

The Texaco station, along the Glenn Highway, was in the middle of Eagle River. Behind, and to the left of the building, the Phillipses had a small building out of which they sold both blocks and cubes of ice. During the warmer times in summer, around the Fourth of July, they could not keep up with the demand for ice. (Helen Phillips family collection.)

The Glenn Highway did not have much traffic in the 1960s. Here, two snow machines are racing on the street in front of the Texaco station. Across the road is the Lamp Post Inn and Restaurant. It was a classy place to get a meal during this time period. (Helen Phillips family collection.)

A wrecker is working at the Texaco station during a snowstorm. Snowstorms kept the wrecker drivers very busy. During the 1960s, the new Glenn Highway was built around Eagle River. For a while, the Phillipses were concerned business would slow down because of the bypass. Fortunately for them, that did not happen. (Helen Phillips family collection.)

This view of Chugiak High School was taken from the parking lot during the 1967–1968 school year. The high school was opened in 1964. According to the book *Between Two Rivers: The Growth of Chugiak–Eagle River* by Marjorie Cochrane, the name Chugiak was chosen instead of Eagle River based on a coin toss. (Chugiak–Eagle River Historical Society.)

Crowds of students and staff stand outside the front entrance to Chugiak High School during the 1967–1968 school year. The school is nearly halfway between Chugiak and Eagle River. Most students had to take the bus to get to the school. (Chugiak–Eagle River Historical Society.)

In this view looking along the Glenn Highway, the Pippel house can be seen to the north. To the right of the house, a United Building Supply business would be built. Later, the lumberyard was replaced by a gas station, which was eventually removed for a Walgreens. (Helen Phillips family collection.)

This photograph was taken in the mid- to late 1960s at the Texaco station. Later on, a McDonald's and a Chevron station would be built at this location. The Parkgate Building would be constructed across the street, close to the two buildings shown. In the background are the Chugach Mountains, with Hiland Mountain to the left. (Helen Phillips family collection.)

A snow machine rider demonstrates a popular winter pastime in Eagle River. Before Pippel's Field was developed, many riders took their snow machines for a spin around the field in the winter months. (Helen Phillips family collection.)

Vernon and Billie Moore purchased this house and 20 acres from Johnnie Johnson in 1959. It was located at about mile three of what is now Eagle River Road. The land was part of a 160-acre homestead settled by Johnnie and Sally Johnson. Billie was instrumental in starting the Eagle River Public Library in 1965. (Chugiak–Eagle River Historical Society.)

This photograph was taken during snowfall on the Glenn Highway to the north of the Texaco station. The house in the photograph, behind the truck, is the yellow Pippel house, which was at the corner of the Eagle River Loop Road and the Glenn Highway. (Helen Phillips family collection.)

The photographer is looking out from under the eaves of the Texaco station at a wrecker with a snowplow clearing the parking lot of the Lamp Post Inn. During the first major snowfall of every winter, the wreckers got a lot of business pulling cars out of the ditches. (Helen Phillips family collection.)

Five

CHANGES BROUGHT BY
THE ALASKA PIPELINE
1970–1980

The 1970s began with the formation of the Chugach State Park. At the time, it was the largest state park in the nation and, to some extent, put a limit on how much Eagle River development could expand. In 1971, Lee Jordan established the *Chugiak–Eagle River Star*, a weekly newspaper. Three years later, in 1974, some of the population was unhappy being part of the Greater Anchorage Area Borough and formed a new borough. Lee Jordan was elected as the first mayor of the Chugiak–Eagle River Borough. He held the office for only a few months before the courts ruled the area could not separate from the Greater Anchorage Area Borough. The next year, the City of Anchorage and the Greater Anchorage Area Borough were combined to form the Municipality of Anchorage, and Eagle River permanently became part of the municipality.

Two major changes occurred in Eagle River in 1973, which would transform the area. The Parkgate Building was opened and was one of the first local buildings with office space, and Dick Rapp, a land speculator, purchased 90 acres of Pippel's Field. Most of the results would not be seen until the 1980s, but the face of Eagle River was changing rapidly.

Important developments were taking place that would change the state of Alaska and Eagle River forever. At the end of the 1960s, the Prudhoe Bay Oilfield was discovered on the North Slope. Construction of the Alaska Pipeline to transfer the oil from Prudhoe Bay to Valdez, where it could be loaded onto tankers, was begun in 1974. The project was completed in 1977 and cost around $8 billion. Thousands of workers had come up to help build the pipeline and work in the new oilfields. Many families moved into Eagle River, and new subdivisions were built. In the 1970s, the Glenn Highway from Eagle River to Anchorage was widened from two to four lanes.

During the decade, hang gliders descended from Mount Baldy to either Pippel's Field in the summer or Fire Lake in the winter. Hang gliding became so popular that the state championships were held in Eagle River.

The picture shows Chugiak High School from the Glenn Highway in 1970. Between the highway and the school was the football field. A larger field, complete with bleachers and a track, was built to the right later. Mount McKinley can be seen on the horizon. (Chugiak–Eagle River Historical Society.)

In 1970, the Eagle River Shopping Center had been extended. To the left, the 76 gas station has been built. More trailers have been parked in the lots behind the center. (First Baptist Church of Eagle River.)

The Eagle River Shopping Center was opened in 1956. This shows the expansion to the right of the original shopping center. The photograph was taken toward the end of the 1960s or in the early 1970s. (Chugiak–Eagle River Historical Society.)

In the distance, between the south end of the Eagle River Shopping Center and the 76 gas station, the first Eagle River Bowl can be seen. This building has been used by a variety of businesses over the years. Since 1988, it has been owned by the First Baptist Church of Eagle River and used for classrooms and a fellowship hall. (Chugiak–Eagle River Historical Society.)

Soon after the Parkgate Building opened in 1973, this photograph was taken. Across the street, to the right, is the Tastee Freez. It has not been open for a number of years. Part of Pippel's Field is at the bottom of the photograph. (Chugiak–Eagle River Historical Society.)

Behind the Texaco station, a moose is seen in Pippel's Field during the early 1970s. Moose are still frequently seen in all areas of Eagle River. Many gardeners have become frustrated trying to keep them from eating their gardens. In the spring, moose calves are often delivered in people's yards. (Helen Phillips family collection.)

This shows a photographer's view of part of Eagle River that was taken after 1973. On the far left along the Old Glenn Highway is the Pippel house. Toward the center is the Parkgate Building. The old Texaco station, owned by the Phillips family, is seen on the field side of the Old Glenn Highway. (Chugiak–Eagle River Historical Society.)

Across Eagle River valley, along the side of Hiland Mountain, Bernie Steward homesteaded. In the 1970s, he had a dirt racetrack on his property. He also ran a small sawmill there. (Chugiak–Eagle River Historical Society.)

This is Paradise Lodge, located at the end of Eagle River Road. The lodge was later changed into a nature center that is currently run by volunteers. People can hike on the original Iditarod Trail or some of the shorter trails in the area. In the center is Polar Bear Peak. (Chugiak–Eagle River Historical Society.)

Located 12 miles from downtown Eagle River was Paradise Lodge. It was later used as the visitors center for Chugach State Park. The park is one of the largest state parks in the nation. It encompasses the mountains on both sides of Eagle River valley as well as most of the land between Turnagain and Knik Arms. (Chugiak–Eagle River Historical Society.)

By 1975, the Glenn Highway no longer ran through Eagle River but around it. It did not affect the businesses in Eagle River much. On the far right of the image is part of the North Slope Restaurant. (First Baptist Church of Eagle River.)

In this view looking east toward Eagle River, one can see how the town is expanding. The New Glenn Highway is prominent in the lower part of the image. Monte Drive is in the center, with the First Baptist Church of Eagle River next to it. Farther to the right is the Eagle River Elementary School. The photograph shows how many areas were heavily wooded close to downtown. (Chugiak–Eagle River Historical Society.)

In 1976, Vern Phillips used his semitruck to pull a bicentennial float for the Chugiak–Eagle River Bicentennial Commission. The float won first prize during the Fur Rendezvous Parade in Anchorage. (Helen Phillips family collection.)

Seen on the left of the photograph, the Eagle River Loop Road meets the Old Glenn Highway. The old post office is to the right of the Parkgate Building and across the Old Glenn Highway from the power substation. (Chugiak–Eagle River Historical Society.)

The Parkgate Building held many businesses in the mid-1980s. The names of those located inside can be seen on the sign. When it was opened in July 1973, the building was one of the first multistory steel buildings in Alaska. It was built with three inches of foam to fill in the space between the steel outside and a finished interior surface. (Chugiak–Eagle River Historical Society.)

This shows construction on one of the subdivisions in Eagle River during the 1970s. When work began on the Trans-Alaska Pipeline in 1974, Eagle River began to grow at a faster pace. There were many families who came to Eagle River at this time. Quite a few decided to stay and are still represented in the community. (Chugiak–Eagle River Historical Society.)

The Alaska Mutual Bank occupied the north end of the Parkgate Building for a number of years. When this picture was taken, the Lamp Post Inn could still be seen to the left. (Chugiak–Eagle River Historical Society.)

Alaska Mutual Bank would, just a few years later in 1987, be forced to merge with United Bank to form the Alliance Bank. This bank would eventually fold in 1989, during the recession, as several other banks in the state had to do. (Chugiak–Eagle River Historical Society.)

In the late 1970s and early 1980s during the winter, hang gliders would land on frozen Fire Lake. In the summer, the state hang gliding championships were held in Eagle River. They would take off from Mount Baldy and land in Pippel's Field. (Helen Phillips family collection.)

When the Carrs Mall was first built, National Bank of Alaska's location was at one end. In the second building of the mall complex, Shakey's Pizza Parlor occupied the right side. Shakey's was a pizza franchise that had stores in several locations around Anchorage before going out of business. (Archie Boyles's collection.)

Six

BOOM YEARS AND DEVELOPMENT OF PIPPEL'S FIELD
1980–1990

The 1980s started out with explosive growth in Eagle River. McDonald's, the first fast-food restaurant of the area, opened in 1981. A traffic light was installed in town for the first time. The US post office was moved from its location at the corner of Coronado Road and the Old Glenn Highway to a spot along the newly created Business Boulevard in 1983. Development in the former Pippel's Field, which had started at the end of the 1970s, really increased with Hickel Construction building two large complexes and a movie theater in 1985.

At the Lions Park along Eagle River Road, the Highland Games started in 1981. The games featured Scottish sporting events and also presented an opportunity to learn about the clans and listen to the bagpipers.

China Lights Restaurant opened in the Regional Park Plaza in 1984. The next year, Garcia's Cantina and Café started business in the Valley River Office Center. In 1970, the Chugiak–Eagle River Chamber of Commerce was formed. In 1986, the chamber began holding the annual Bear Paw Festival the second weekend of July. The festival has grown into one of the largest events in the area and draws people from all over to take part in the many activities.

Unfortunately, a downturn in the economy began in the middle of the decade. The recession that had started in the Lower 48 arrived in Alaska and hit the Anchorage area especially hard. In 1987, almost 20,000 people left the Anchorage area, and real estate values dropped. Several banks in the area closed, and competition for jobs was fierce.

Some roads in Eagle River were paved and had improvements made to them. When the economy got better near the end of the decade, there was talk of extending the Eagle River Loop Road to connect with Hiland Road and the Glenn Highway. This would provide another route out of town and relieve some of the congestion in downtown Eagle River during the commuting hours.

In the mid-1980s, chamber of commerce volunteers planted flowers along Chief Alex Park, but not the larger trees and bushes that would come later. The orange 76 station ball was still a familiar sight on the Old Glenn Highway. The First Baptist Church of Eagle River had a bus ministry. (Archie Boyles's collection.)

In this view looking down the big hill on Eagle River Loop Road, Mount Susitna can be seen on the horizon. There are still woods along the left side of the road going down the hill. Occasionally, the police have had to close this part of the road due to ice. (Archie Boyles's collection.)

Standing in the Carrs Mall parking lot, one can see the post office near the flagpole. It was opened at this location in 1983. In the far left of the mall was the National Bank of Alaska. The sign for the Book Cache store in the mall can be seen as well. (Archie Boyles's collection.)

The family that owned Eagle River Duck Pond Car Wash used to keep geese and peacocks at the pond. Here, a family is feeding some of the birds in the winter. The wooden deck allows people to feed the birds year-round. (Chugiak–Eagle River Historical Society.)

Many birds are seen feeding at the duck pond. The pond is a popular place to feed the birds and have picnics. It is located near the north end of town and easy to get to. (Archie Boyles's collection.)

Eagle River is along the path of migration for several species of birds. The duck pond attracts many waterfowl in the spring and fall. In the fall, it is not unusual to see large flocks of Canada geese flying above town making their way south. (Archie Boyles's collection.)

The overlook at the duck pond is near where a stream comes in to replenish the water. It is not a natural pond, but one that was built to take advantage of the little stream that runs through the north part of town. It was originally built and operated by Larry and Sharon Thomas. (Chugiak–Eagle River Historical Society.)

The building started here would eventually house the Chugiak–Eagle River Branch Library, Garcia's Cantina & Café, and several other city and private offices. This area used to be known as Pippel's Field. In 1984, due to money pouring into the state from the Alaska Pipeline, the open areas around town started filling in with subdivisions and businesses. (Archie Boyles's collection.)

Hickel Construction has just started building on land that used to be part of Pippel's Field. When completed, this building was one of two the company constructed with distinct blue roofs. It also built the Valley River Cinemas to the left of this image. The light poles show where Business Boulevard would be. (Archie Boyles's collection.)

A large amount of construction occurred along Business Boulevard in 1985. On the right, workers are building on property that would be called the Valley River Office Center. Some of the businesses that have operated out of this building include a travel agency, tanning salon, and dentist's office. (Archie Boyles's collection.)

This is shortly after the building was completed in 1985. The library has already moved into the second floor, leaving its old location at the north end of the Eagle River Shopping Center. Garcia's Cantina & Café occupied the space below the library in the center of the building, and across the street an office building has just been completed as well. (Archie Boyles's collection.)

In the 1970s and 1980s, the Eagle River Laundry occupied the building next to the First Baptist Church. On the other side of the large parking lot, to the left of the church, is a trailer court that was a fixture in town for many years. (Archie Boyles's collection.)

The Regional Park Plaza at the north end of the old Pippel's Field is shown here. In this image taken soon after the mall opened in 1984, the original businesses' signs can be seen. China Lights Restaurant and TCBY were at one end of the mall, with JANA's video and Matanuska Telephone Association (MTA) at the other end. MTA still has its offices here, while many other businesses in the Regional Park Plaza have come and gone. In the middle was a Laundromat. (Archie Boyles's collection.)

China Lights Restaurant was one of the first businesses in the strip mall when it opened in 1984. TCBY and Mailboxes Etc. were other tenants in the mall at that time as well. (Archie Boyles's collection.)

The image above was taken from Farm Avenue and shows the construction of the Eagle River Bowl in 1985. Pictured below, the bowling alley has 24 lanes, a snack bar, and a video arcade. The building also has a lounge and laundry mat. It is located across from the Eagle River Commons Park. (Both, Archie Boyles's collection.)

This construction is in the early 1980s of the Eagle River Motel. It is located near the Old Eagle River Road, across the street from Chief Alex Park. (First Baptist Church of Eagle River.)

The Matanuska Credit Union and Eagle River Community Office building on Business Boulevard is shown in the late 1980s or early 1990s. The hill behind the building was developed as part of the Eagle River Commons Park, located in the center of Eagle River. Looking north from the picnic spot, Mount McKinley can be seen on a clear day. To the east is a great view of the mountains on both sides of Eagle River valley. (Chugiak–Eagle River Chamber of Commerce.)

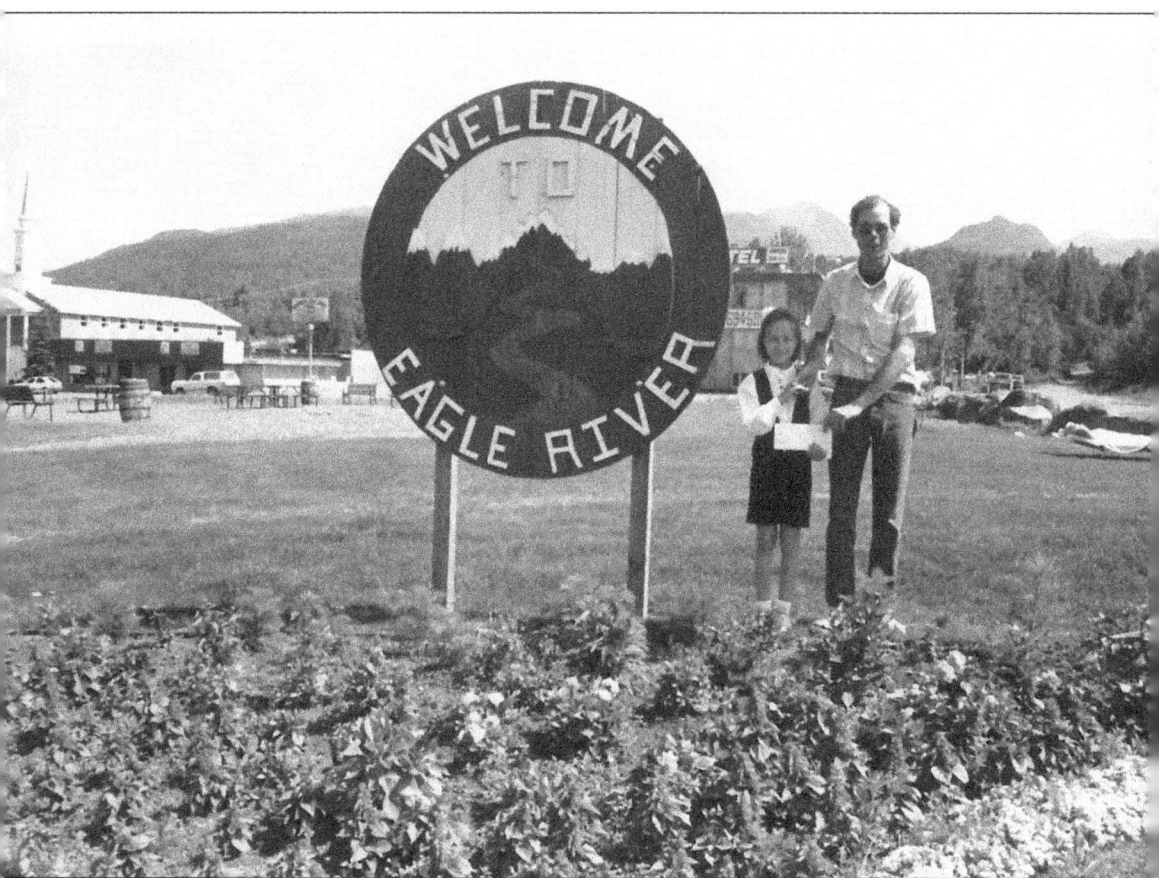

The old Eagle River sign in Chief Alex Park welcomed people to Eagle River during the 1980s. The woods in the area had been cut down to create the park. It was several years before trees grew up in the park again. (Chugiak–Eagle River Chamber of Commerce.)

The old Tastee Freez structure and a sign listing businesses in the Parkgate Building are shown. Many businesses have come and gone, but a few, like the motor vehicle and driver licenses and the barbershop, have stayed for several decades. (Chugiak–Eagle River Historical Society.)

A fixture in the community for a number of years, the Tastee Freez had to close its doors in the 1980s. The building and lot have stayed untouched since the closing of the Tastee Freez. (Chugiak–Eagle River Historical Society.)

Zales and the Book Cache occupied this part of the Carrs Mall in the early 1980s. The Book Cache was a bookstore chain in Alaska and a couple of other states, which reached its peak in 1983. By the 1990s, the chain started closing stores due to competition from Waldenbooks and B. Dalton. (Archie Boyles's collection.)

The Alaska Highland Games have been held at the grounds of the Eagle River Lions Club since 1981. This 1986 photograph shows part of the band competition sponsored by The Glenlivet Scotch. It is still held during the first weekend of August every year. (Chugiak–Eagle River Chamber of Commerce.)

Bagpipers are a popular attraction during the Highland Games in Eagle River. The Lions Club has leased the 40 acres from the state since 1962. Over the years, the Lions have built a number of ball fields, a basketball court, several tennis courts, and picnic spots on the property. (Chugiak–Eagle River Chamber of Commerce.)

The Highland Games in Eagle River are more than just athletic events. The games allow mingling with others from one's clan and indulging in Scottish culture. Here is a band competition from one of the earlier years. (Chugiak–Eagle River Chamber of Commerce.)

Miss Bear Paw rides on a float in the Fur Rendezvous Parade in Anchorage. Even though the Fur Rendezvous is held in February, a big part of Miss Bear Paw's duties is to drum up interest for the Bear Paw Festival. (Chugiak–Eagle River Chamber of Commerce.)

A vintage fire truck from Fort Richardson Army Base is getting ready for the Bear Paw Parade. On the hill behind the truck is McDonald's, the first fast-food restaurant in Eagle River. It opened in 1981. (Chugiak–Eagle River Chamber of Commerce.)

This is the start of the Bear Paw Classic 5K Race during the Bear Paw Festival, probably taken in the late 1980s or early 1990s. It remains a popular race for runners, drawing people from all over the Anchorage area and beyond. (Chugiak–Eagle River Chamber of Commerce.)

The float for the University of Alaska–Anchorage Eagle River extension passes by during Bear Paw. University of Alaska–Anchorage started offering higher-education courses in the Eagle River area in 1976. The number of University of Alaska–Anchorage classes has increased over the years, with many of the classes being offered in the evenings. (Chugiak–Eagle River Chamber of Commerce.)

One of the more unique contests held at the Bear Paw Festival draws a crowd. The Slippery Salmon Olympics involves navigating a course carrying a serving tray with one hand while holding a real salmon in the other hand. (Chugiak–Eagle River Chamber of Commerce.)

By the 1980s, the Briggses had developed or sold most of their property in the Eagle River area. They still had about 16 acres around Glenn's and Dale's houses near the middle of town. This picture from Mount Baldy shows the part of Eagle River surrounding this area. The large wooden plot in the middle of the photograph shows the area of the two Briggses' family homes. (Archie Boyles's collection.)

This photograph taken from Mount Baldy shows the Eagle River Duck Pond Car Wash near the center. Fred Meyer would be built to the lower right part of the view, and the medical facilities near the duck pond would be constructed later. (Archie Boyles's collection.)

Taken during the winter, toward the end of the 1980s, this image shows the large lot in the center where Walmart would be built in 2000. The Eagle River Loop Road had not been extended yet to meet Hiland Road and the Glenn Highway. Houses at the top of Skyline Drive are in the foreground. (Archie Boyles's collection.)

Eagle River passes under the Glenn Highway Bridge near this spot. On the right is the location of the Eagle River Campground. Just out of sight to the left is where Meadow Creek enters the river. A few houses are also nearby on the left side. Often during the winter, when the cold air settles, this can be one of the coldest areas in town. (Chugiak–Eagle River Chamber of Commerce.)

First Baptist Church of Eagle River can be seen near the center of the photograph. Across the street is St. Andrew Catholic Church. The gravel pit where a new Catholic church building would later be constructed can be seen on the other side of the Glenn Highway. (Archie Boyles's collection.)

Blockbuster's first location in Eagle River was on Business Boulevard near the Eagle River Bowl. This was taken before the Pet Zoo was built to the right of Blockbuster. By the 1990s, there were fewer open spots in the former Pippel's Field. (Archie Boyles's collection.)

The Valley River Center was built in 1985 and contained the Pay 'n Save and Safeway stores. This building was part of the Hickel Construction complex in downtown Eagle River. Eventually, the part of the building containing Safeway was remodeled and called the Eagle River Town Center. Several city offices and the public library were relocated to this section. (Archie Boyles's collection.)

This picture of the Pippel Mall was taken from across Business Boulevard, in the Carrs's parking lot in the 1980s. In the early 1980s, growth in Eagle River changed rapidly due to oil money after the completion of the Alaska Pipeline. The population of the area increased about fivefold between 1970 and 1990. (Archie Boyles's collection.)

Taken during the fall of 1988, this image shows Joy Lutheran Church, with Mount Baldy in the distance. In the following years, a new sanctuary was added to the building. (First Baptist Church of Eagle River.)

David Morris is shown here during his senior year in 1988. He is between Dean Fleer (left) and Richard Lee. In 1999, in Chicago, David Morris set the official US record for the marathon. He covered the 26.2-mile course in 2 hours, 9 minutes, and 32 seconds. (Chugiak–Eagle River Historical Society.)

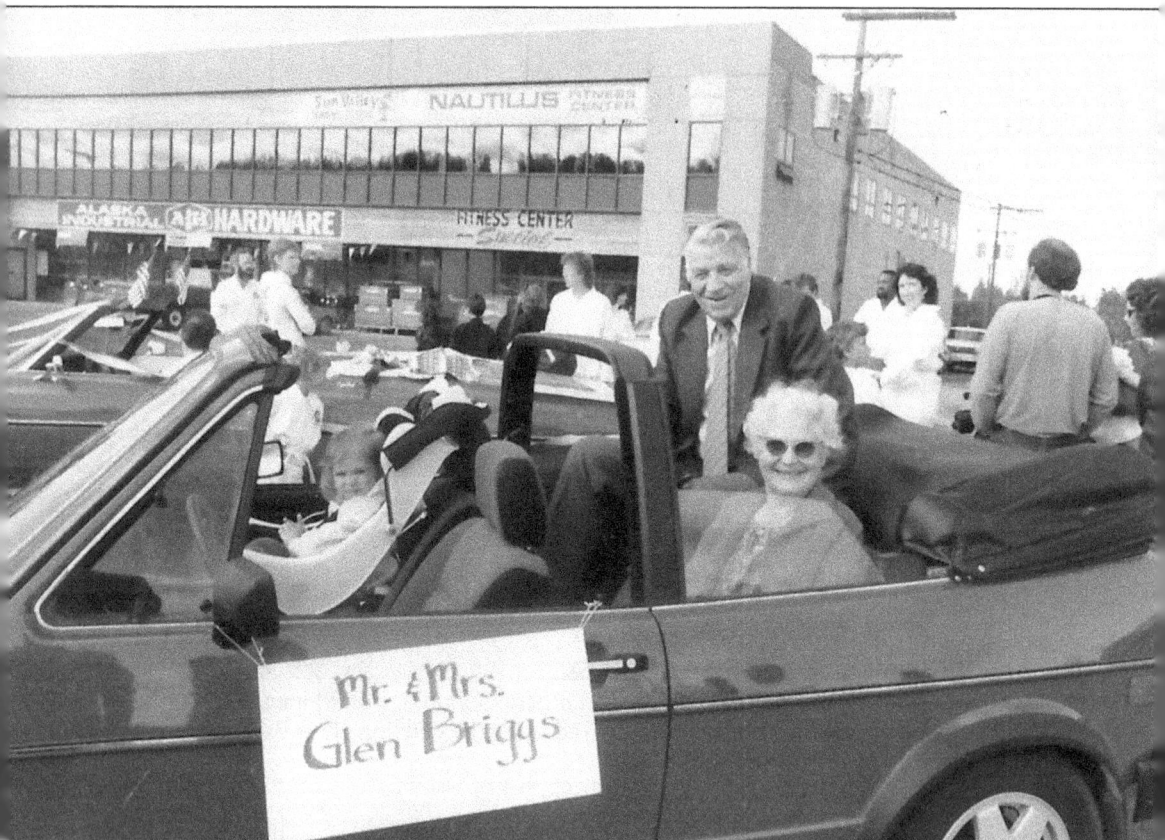

Glenn and Mary Lou Briggs are getting ready for a ride in the Bear Paw Parade. Glenn was Eagle River's first assemblyman when the Greater Anchorage Borough was formed in 1963. He passed away in May 1990. (Chugiak–Eagle River Historical Society.)

The North Slope Restaurant started in 1971 in a trailer. Eventually, the owner built a larger, fancier place designed with a Western theme. The photograph was taken from the restaurant's parking lot. (Archie Boyles's collection.)

Eagle River saw a great increase in auto parts stores in the area. This photograph shows the Grand Auto Parts store being constructed. The building would later be taken over by the Speedy Auto Glass business on one side and Jazzercise on the other. (Archie Boyles's collection.)

Man O' War Road is being paved in the fall of 1988. Many of the older streets of Eagle River were hard-surfaced for the first time in the 1980s. Man O' War Road was part of a subdivision with streets that Danny Bell named after famous racehorses. Other streets were named Citation, Whirlaway, Twenty Grand, Sun Beau, and War Admiral. (Author's collection.)

The view from Hiland Road shows Eagle River Loop Road ending just before the river. In this part of town, 42 houses were moved as the road was widened and extended across the river. This would connect the Loop Road to Hiland Road and the Glenn Highway. This additional route to Anchorage helped with traffic congestion during peak commuting times. (Author's collection.)

Seven

More Recent Times
1990–Present

The Briggs Bridge was opened in 1992. It was named for Glenn Briggs, an Eagle River pioneer who had passed away in May 1990. Glenn always thought it was in Eagle River's best interest to be part of Anchorage. He probably would have been pleased knowing this bridge, which allows better access to Anchorage, was named after him.

In 1993, Walmart purchased a large lot that was formerly part of Danny Bell's homestead. Due to opposition from the neighbors and the corporation being distracted by expansion in Canada, a Walmart store was not opened until 2000. Another large store, Fred Meyer, was built on the other side of Eagle River. Between the two, residents did not have to go to Anchorage as often to purchase items.

The large shopping complex that used to hold the Pay 'n Save and Safeway stores, as well as a few other smaller shops, was converted into the Eagle River Town Center in 2009. Half of the building houses the Alaska Club, and the other half houses city offices, the Chugiak–Eagle River Chamber of Commerce, and the Chugiak–Eagle River Branch Library. Across the street from the complex is the Eagle River Commons Park. A little farther down the street, Eagle River Town Square Park has picnic tables and an ice-skating area.

In the winter of 2011–2012, a new snowfall accumulation record for one season was set in the Anchorage area. The official tally was 133.6 inches, or just over 11 feet.

Eagle River has come a long way in a short number of years. Most of the early homesteaders are gone, but new generations have grown to love the area. What will the future hold for the next generation in Eagle River?

In October 1992, Gov. Wally Hickel gave a speech to dedicate the Briggs Bridge. The bridge gave Eagle River residents another way to the Glenn Highway. Danny Bell had blazed a trail in the 1970s along the route used for the road, but at the time, the city did not appreciate his work. (Chugiak–Eagle River Historical Society.)

Mary Lou Briggs is getting ready to break the bottle to signal the opening of the new bridge over Eagle River. At her side is Gov. Wally Hickel, who had wanted to build up the infrastructure of Alaska. Even though this project started before he came into office for the second time, he appears to enjoy opening a new road in Alaska. The man at left is unidentified. (Chugiak–Eagle River Historical Society.)

The Bear Paw Parade has become so well attended over the years that patrons need to get along the route early to find prime viewing spots. Kids like to watch near the sidelines since the people in the parade toss candy or small gifts to them. It is a great time to run into friends. (Chugiak–Eagle River Chamber of Commerce.)

The Rotten Sneaker contest at Bear Paw is another popular event during the festival. Here, the judges are making their decision. (Chugiak–Eagle River Chamber of Commerce.)

Two moose are standing in a pond along Eagle River Road. This shallow pond is a prime spot to see moose feeding in the early-morning or evening hours. On the way to the nature center, it is on the right near the river. (Author's collection.)

Taken while standing on frozen Eagle River, this image shows Briggs Bridge in the early part of the 1990s. Snow-machiners like to travel up and down on the ice during winter months. A greenbelt is along most of the river. (Author's collection.)

Two of the attractions at the Bear Paw Festival each year include carnival rides and the classic car show. The carnival rides are set up on the Eagle River Commons Park along Business Boulevard. The classic car show gives car owners a chance to display their restored or purchased vehicles. (Chugiak–Eagle River Chamber of Commerce.)

As seen in this photograph, the Bear Paw Classic 5K has become one of the main events of the festival. People of all ages compete in the race. This part of the race runs down Business Boulevard in the middle of Eagle River. There is plenty of room for people to watch on both sides of the road. (Chugiak–Eagle River Chamber of Commerce.)

One of the other main events at the Bear Paw Festival is the choosing of the Bear Paw Court. During the parade, the court rides in cars or on floats, depending on the year. The court helps promote the different activities around town. (Chugiak–Eagle River Chamber of Commerce.)

Pack No. 219 of the Cub Scouts carries a banner during the Bear Paw Parade. This shows the group in the 1990s. Scouts have made many contributions to the community of Eagle River. Some of the furniture in the Chugiak–Eagle River Branch Library was created and donated by Boy Scouts as Eagle Scout projects. (Chugiak–Eagle River Chamber of Commerce.)

Chugiak High School is easy to see in this photograph taken from Mount Baldy in the late 1980s or early 1990s. The Steve Primis auditorium and the library have been built, and there are several portables in front of the school. This was before Eagle River High School was opened in 2005. (Archie Boyles's collection.)

While the photographer was floating down from the North Fork of Eagle River, this moose was seen. To float Eagle River, a person puts in at the North Fork recreational area and takes out at Briggs Bridge before the rapids. In *Shem Pete's Alaska*, the author talks about the Dena'ina Indians hunting for moose in the upper parts of Eagle River valley. After killing a number of moose, the Indians would build a raft and float back down the river with the meat. (Author's collection.)

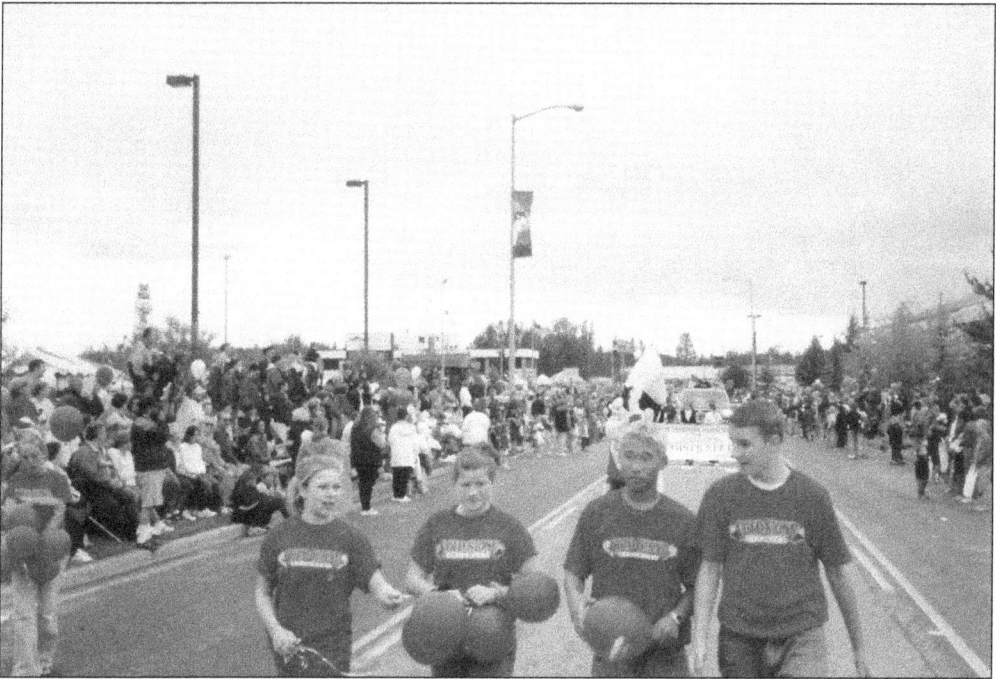

Several individuals in the Bear Paw Parade advertise for the Cold Stone Creamery with their T-shirts. People are lined on both sides of Business Boulevard to watch the parade. The parade has grown into the biggest event of Bear Paw and draws people from all over to watch. (Chugiak–Eagle River Chamber of Commerce.)

The Dena'ina Indians from Eklutna are the largest private landowners in the Municipality of Anchorage. In the 1990s, they started developing the Powder Ridge subdivision, seen in this view looking down from Mount Baldy. (Archie Boyles's collection.)

Eagle River valley is viewed from the ridge above the nature center. According to Mendenhall's report, his party traveled down this part of the valley on the left, or south, side. (Author's collection.)

In 1996, Pippel's Field was well on its way to being completely developed. At the top of the photograph is First National Bank Alaska, which had opened a branch across from the Eagle River Shopping Center in the late 1970s. To the right, across Business Boulevard, the Carrs Mall and its complex had gone in about the same time. (First Baptist Church of Eagle River.)

One of the largest events to take place in the Chugiak–Eagle River area was the 1996 Arctic Winter Games. Over 1,500 athletes and coaches from all around the world, who live north of the 55th parallel, gathered to compete in the games. (Chugiak–Eagle River Chamber of Commerce.)

Running is a popular sport and recreational activity in the area. The local high schools have had many successful track and cross-country squads. Many people proudly wear their T-shirts from the Bear Paw Classic 5K Race throughout the year. (Chugiak–Eagle River Chamber of Commerce.)

During the Bear Paw Festival, a couple of members of the Bear Paw Court are trying their hands at one of the racing games. This event is taking place in the large parking lot of the Valley River Cinemas. This open area is filled with vendors and numerous activities during the days of the Bear Paw Festival. (Chugiak–Eagle River Chamber of Commerce.)

A float made by the Chugiak Jr. and Sr. Mushing Club is shown during the Bear Paw Parade, around 1990. Mushing is a popular sport in the area. Beach Lake has a number of trails used by the dog sled teams. In the past, the Eagle River Classic Dog Sled Race has been held at this location. (Chugiak–Eagle River Chamber of Commerce.)

Joe Redington is coming up the hill to Checkpoint No. 1. Joe is 80 years old in this photograph. He is considered the "Father of the Iditarod." Redington's best finish was fifth place, which he accomplished in 1975, 1977, 1978, and 1988. (VFW Post No. 9785.)

Joe Redington stops at Checkpoint No. 1 in 1997. Joe was running as musher No. 1 in honor of his contribution to the forming of the Iditarod race. He was racing at age 80 that year, after taking the previous four years off. (VFW Post No. 9785.)

A dog team comes up the hill to Checkpoint No. 1 in Eagle River. At the bottom of the hill is where the teams cross the ice of Eagle River. This photograph is from the race in 1997. There were only two years between 1971 and 2000 that part of the trail from Anchorage to Eagle River was not run due to icy conditions and lack of snow. (VFW Post No. 9785.)

Martin Buser is arriving in Eagle River with his dog team during the Iditarod race. By 1997, he was one of the more popular mushers, winning the Iditarod in 1992 and 1994. Between 1986 and 1997, he finished in the top 10 of every race. (VFW Post No. 9785.)

DeeDee Jonrowe is pulling into Checkpoint No. 1. She is a very popular musher from Willow. She continued to participate in the Iditarod after dealing with cancer. DeeDee was voted most inspirational musher in 1993 and finished second that year. At the time of this photograph, in 1997, she had nine straight top-10 finishes. (VFW Post No. 9785.)

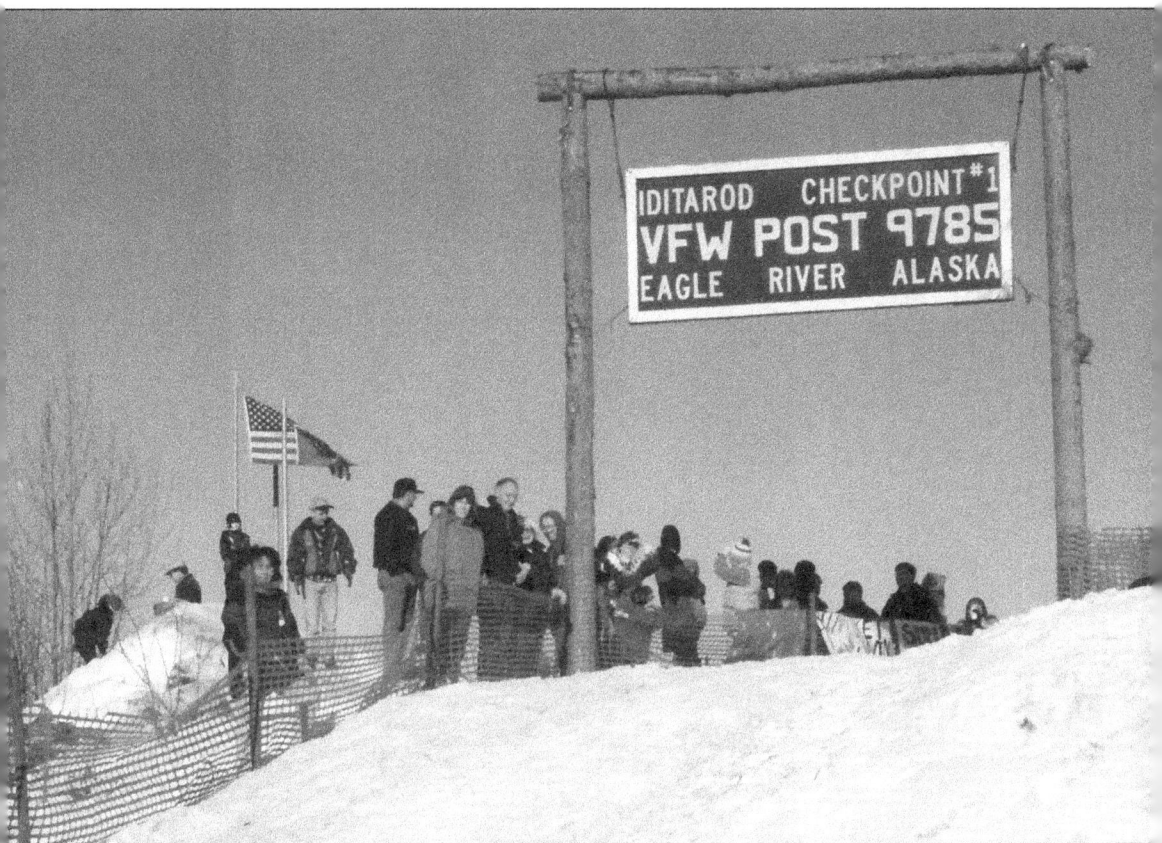

For the first 29 years of the Iditarod race, the VFW Post No. 9785 was the first checkpoint. This shows the steep climb up to the sign and into the VFW parking lot. From the parking lot, the dog teams were then loaded into their trucks and hauled to Wasilla or Willow for the restart of the race, depending on the trail conditions. (VFW Post No. 9785.)

A musher smiles as he pulls into Checkpoint No. 1. Along the chute, handmade signs cheer the mushers on. Many spectators come out every year to watch the race. In the early years of the race, the portion between Anchorage and Eagle River counted in the total time for the Iditarod. The mushers would then load their dogs and quickly get to the restart area either in Wasilla or Willow. (VFW Post No. 9785.)

To check the trail conditions between Anchorage and Eagle River, the Anchorage Police Department drove snow machines along the trail. This officer is coming into Checkpoint No. 1 after monitoring the trail for hazards to the mushers in 1998. (VFW Post No. 9785.)

Ramey Redington pulls into the parking lot at the VFW Post No. 9785. He is getting ready to load his dogs and sled to transport them to the restart in Wasilla, 40 miles away. Checkpoint No. 1 at Eagle River was so close to Anchorage, it was a very popular place for spectators to watch the Iditarod race. Most of the trail goes through remote parts of Alaska with few viewing opportunities. (VFW Post No. 9785.)

The parking area behind VFW Post No. 9785 is where the dog teams were loaded for the drive to the restart area. Mushers customize their trucks so each dog has its own compartment, and there is room for the sled. Sometimes, the mushers give each dog its own nameplate on its compartment. (VFW Post No. 9785.)

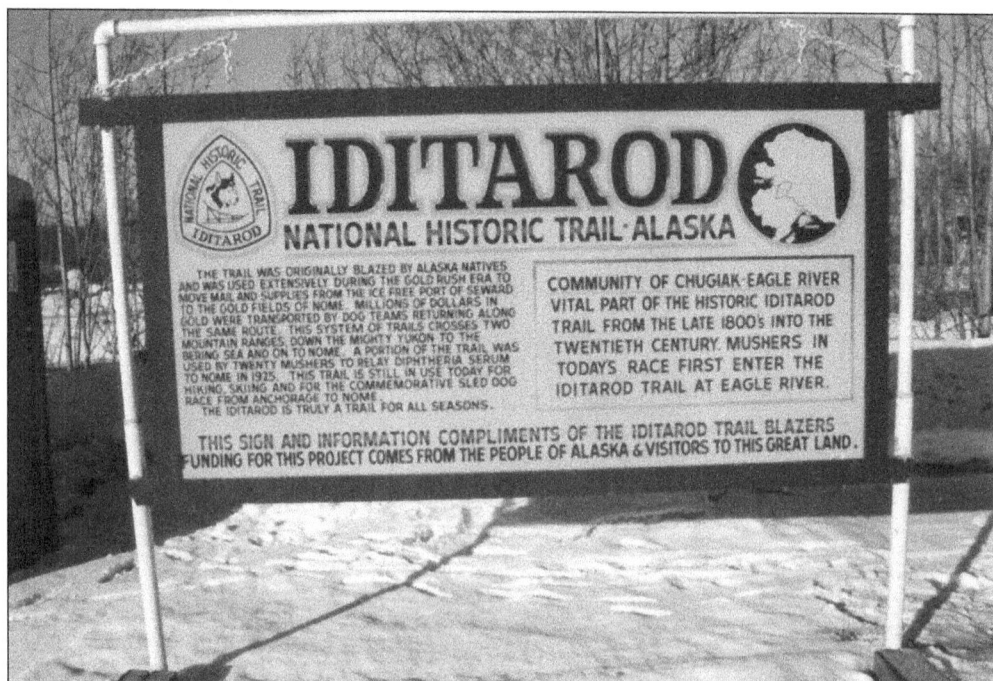

The Iditarod Trail Blazers erected the sign in front of VFW Post No. 9785. It explains the history of the original Iditarod Trail and the importance of Eagle River as part of the first and the current trails. (VFW Post No. 9785.)

Crowds are waiting for dog teams to arrive at the first checkpoint during the 1998 Iditarod. The Glenn Highway can be seen to the right. The dog teams cross Eagle River and then come up the hill to the VFW parking lot. (VFW Post No. 9785.)

A dog team is pulling into the VFW parking lot to load up and travel to the restart. Across Eagle River Road is the old fire station in the background. Part of the VFW's building is on the left. Mount Baldy is seen on the left of the Chugach Mountains. (VFW Post No. 9785.)

In the distance, Eagle River is emptying into Knik Arm as viewed from Mount Baldy in the early 2000s. During the construction of the railroad in 1915, materials were off-loaded at the mouth of the river to be transported to the work site. (Archie Boyles's collection.)

The landing area for military troops, during parachute training, is west of town toward Knik Arm. Soldiers can often be seen from Eagle River jumping out of C-17s, C-130s, or other aircraft. Both the Air Force and Army are well represented among families living in Eagle River. (Archie Boyles's collection.)

On the left is the steeple of First Baptist Church of Eagle River. Toward the right, a large white roof shows the location of the movie theater. By the year 2000, most of Pippel's Field was filled with houses and businesses. (Archie Boyles's collection.)

When Safeway purchased the Carrs grocery store chain in 1999, it closed the Safeway store and took over the Carrs store in Eagle River. A grocery chain called Alaska Marketplace then used the former location of the Safeway store. The Alaska Marketplace only stayed in business for 14.5 months. (Archie Boyles's collection.)

In the Bear Paw Parade, Corvettes have been well represented through the years. In this photograph, these court members are being given a ride in a new Corvette. This part of the route takes them in front of the Parkgate Building next to the Old Glenn Highway. (Chugiak–Eagle River Chamber of Commerce.)

Parking is a challenge in downtown Eagle River during the Bear Paw Festival. After finding a rare parking spot, the spectators then watch the parade. This year, the parade included the Eagle River Waste Management Department showing off its trucks. (Chugiak–Eagle River Chamber of Commerce.)

From Farm Avenue, houses can be seen on the slopes of Mount Baldy. The Alaska USA Federal Credit Union has been built across the Old Glenn Highway. On the left of Farm Avenue is the Little Red Schoolhouse day care. (Archie Boyles's collection.)

Taken in the early 1990s, this photograph shows the large lot where Walmart would be built. Initially, many people in Eagle River opposed the big-box store moving to the area. After it was built, a person could tell that it was a popular spot to shop by the full parking lot. (Author's collection.)

Kentucky Fried Chicken occupies the south end of the mall complex here in the 1990s. Above the mall on the left is a popular hangout, Sleepy Dog Coffee, Inc. To the right, also with a Western theme, is the top of the North Slope Restaurant. The North Slope Restaurant has been a fixture in Eagle River since 1971. (Archie Boyles's collection.)

In the top left corner are the ice rinks and track for Gruening Junior High School. Just below is King's Way Ministry Center with the new sanctuary. To the right is the large white roof of Homestead Elementary School. In the foreground, Brendalwood subdivision is just beginning to be developed. (Archie Boyles's collection.)

Viewed from Farm Avenue, the dark building on the left held the NAPA store before it moved to a new location farther down the Old Glenn Highway. Behind Schuck's store, residences would eventually be built in 2005. The woods to the right would be cleared for the Alaska USA Federal Credit Union. (Archie Boyles's collection.)

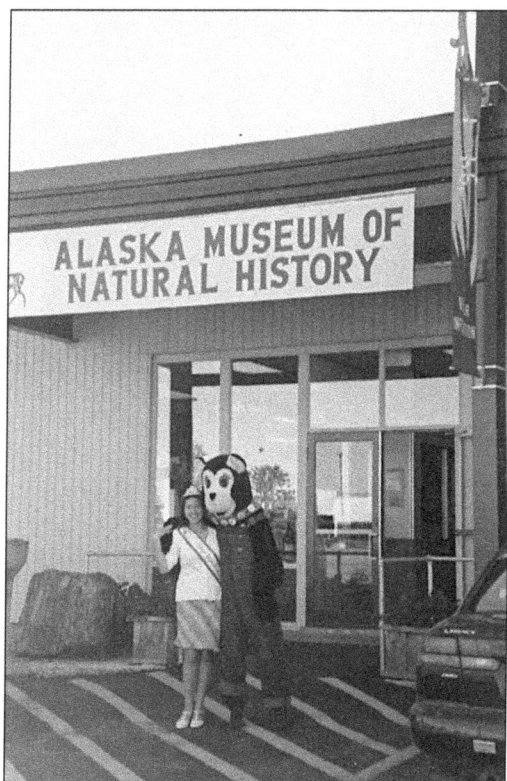

The Alaska Museum of Natural History was located in the Parkgate Building and was highly supported by Mary Lou Briggs. This shows the museum sign with Miss Bear Paw of the year posing under it. (Chugiak–Eagle River Chamber of Commerce.)

The truck is hauling dirt from the Walmart store construction site. Eagle River's Walmart opened in 2000. It was about seven years before the company added onto the store and made it a supercenter. (Archie Boyles's collection.)

Walmart had purchased this land in 1993, but due to opposition to the store and because Walmart was opening several stores in Canada, the Eagle River store was not built until seven years later, in 2000. (Archie Boyles's collection.)

By 2003, the Old Glenn Highway through Eagle River had been turned into a five-lane thoroughfare. The intersection in front of the Eagle River Shopping Center has always been one of the busiest areas of town. (First Baptist Church of Eagle River.)

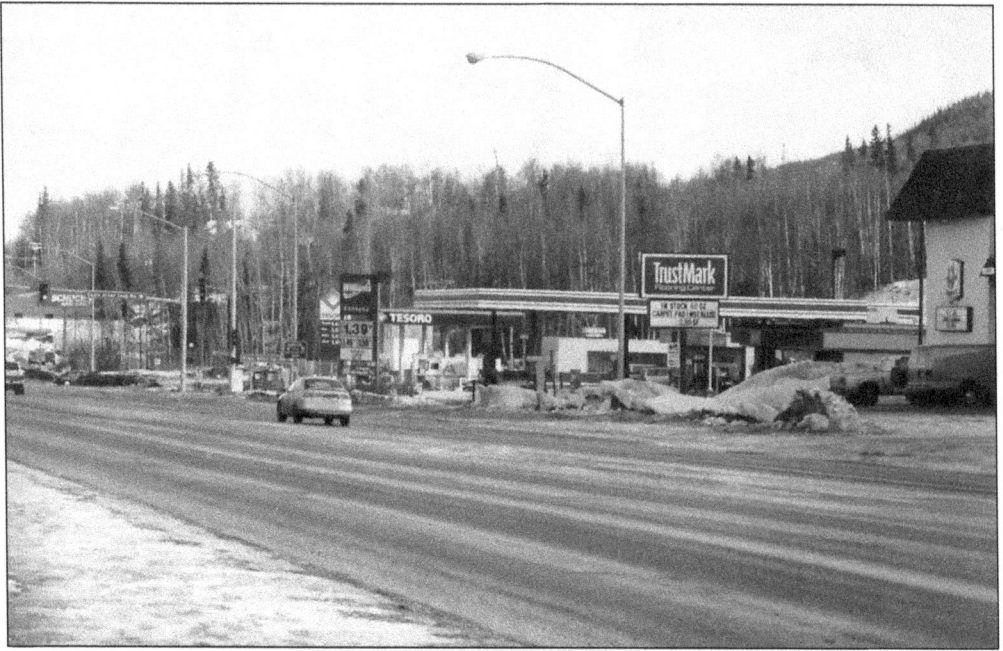

At the corner of Eagle River Loop Road and the Old Glenn Highway was a Williams gas station. This was the old site of the United Builder's Supply lumberyard. Across the Eagle River Loop Road is a Tesoro gas station near where the Pippel house used to be. Take note of the price of gas! (Archie Boyles's collection.)

Construction is beginning on a large house at the top of Skyline Drive. Taken during the early years of the 2000s, this shows Pippel's Field nearly full of buildings. The open land between Business Boulevard and the Glenn Highway would soon contain condos, a Publix Self Storage, and a new Credit Union One building. (Archie Boyles's collection.)

In this view looking down from Mount Baldy, the open area on the right is Schroeder Park, located on End Street. The park was named for the Schroeder family who homesteaded 160 acres in 1954. The street was named End because at one time it was at the end of Farm Avenue. In the 1980s, Farm Avenue was extended beyond End Street toward the Glenn Highway, and many more houses were built. (Archie Boyles's collection.)

In this view looking down from Mount Baldy, the closest building is the Harry J. MacDonald Memorial Center. Fire Lake Elementary School is located just beyond. In the early 2000s, the land below Lower Fire Lake was filling in with development. (Archie Boyles's collection.)

The large body of water at the top of the picture is Knik Arm. Lower Fire Lake, shown in the center, is a popular place for fishing for rainbow trout and northern pike in the summer and winter. It is also frequently used by floatplanes in the summer. (Archie Boyles's collection.)

Looking down from Mount Baldy, one can see that Pippel's Field still has a few areas not developed yet in the late 1990s. Woods still occupy the area that would become Eagle River Commons Park in the center of town. Farm Avenue is toward the right of the photograph and has already been extended beyond End Street. (Archie Boyles's collection.)

This photograph shows that many houses had been built on the slopes of Mount Baldy by the 1990s. The original homesteader was given some ridicule for claiming land that was sloped so much. Eventually, many of the nicer homes in the area were built along Skyline Drive. (Archie Boyles's collection.)

On a clear day, Mount McKinley to the north can be seen from various places in Eagle River. The mountain can be seen even though it is over 130 air miles away. In this view looking from the top of Skyline Drive, the 20,320-foot summit is seen on the right, with the smaller Mount Hunter on the left. (Author's collection.)

In 2006, the new Catholic church building was completed. It is located on a hill across the Glenn Highway from the main part of Eagle River. The structure can be seen from several locations around town and can hold about 1,000 people. (Author's collection.)

Tips Bar has been a landmark location in Eagle River for over five decades. The building also contains Pete's Barbeque. Pete's is known around town for its great burgers. They are located at the corner of Santa Maria Drive and the Old Glenn Highway. (Author's collection.)

At the end of June 2009, the Eagle River Town Center was opened. The former Alaska Marketplace store was remodeled to contain the Chugiak–Eagle River Branch Library, the park and recreation office, a police substation, the Chugiak–Eagle River Chamber of Commerce, and various other offices. The other end of the building holds the Alaska Club. (Author's collection.)

Found at the duck pond near the overlook of the pond, this statue, pictured in 2003, represents the bearded sourdough of Alaska's past. There are still a few individuals around who bear a striking resemblance to those early pioneers. (Helen Phillips family collection.)

Bald eagles are frequently seen around Eagle River. A favorite hangout of theirs during the colder parts of winter is along the lower part of Meadow Creek at the top of cottonwood trees. Occasionally, 15 or more eagles can be seen at one time. (Author's collection.)

One of the best views of the Chugach Mountains is seen going toward Eagle River from the Hiland Exit on the Eagle River Loop Road. During the fall, the yellow colors are spectacular, and during the winter, the mountains are covered in a beautiful coat of snow. (Author's collection.)

In the winter of 2011–12, Anchorage set a record for the greatest accumulation of snow for the area. The picture above shows a scene in the summer. The picture below shows the same location at the end of the winter with record snowfall. The record was set at 133.6 inches, just over 11 feet, surpassing the old record of 132.6 inches set in the winter of 1954–1955. (Both, author's collection.)

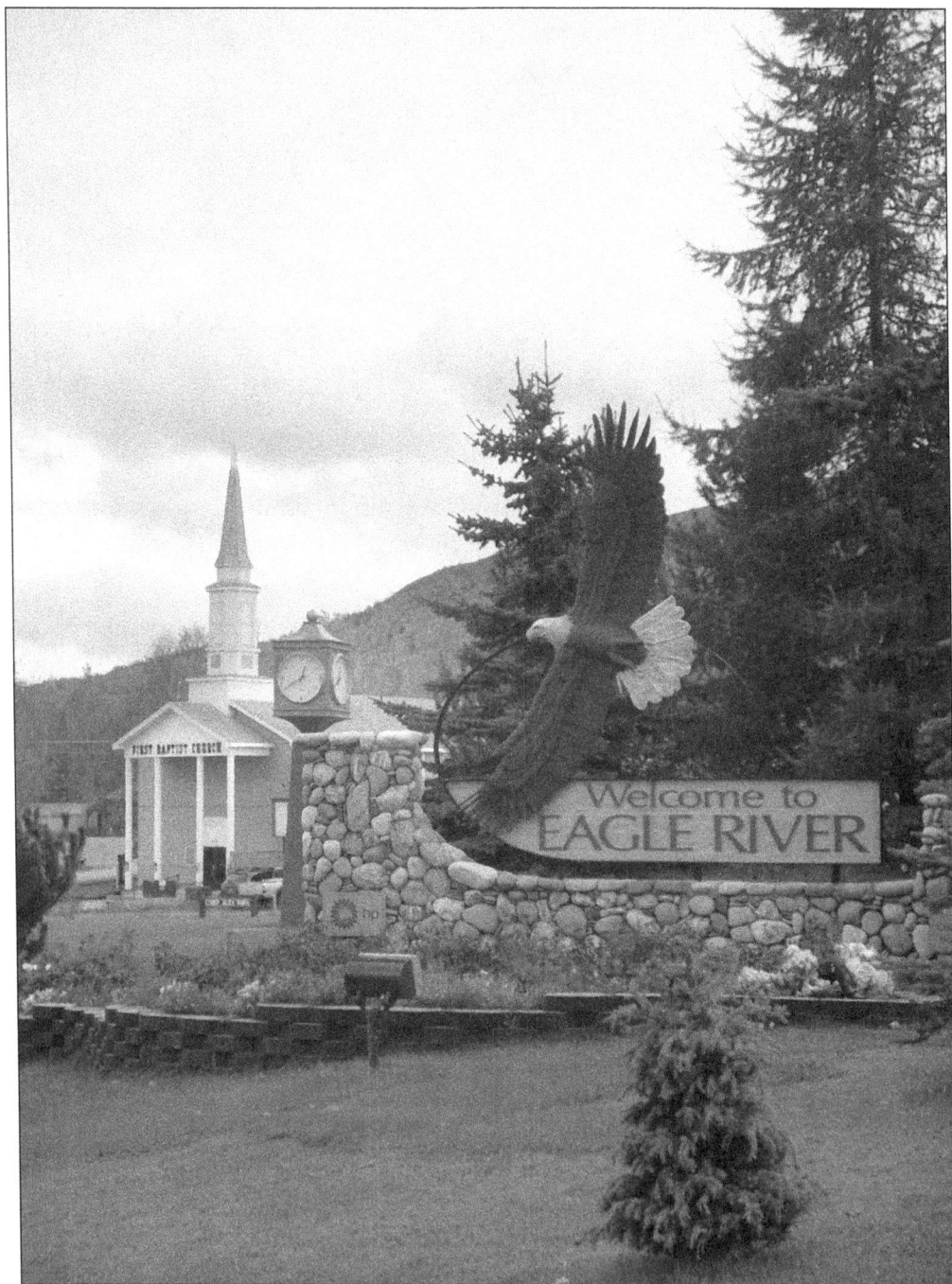

In this view looking across Chief Alex Park in 2012, a new "Welcome to Eagle River" sign and First Baptist Church of Eagle River can be seen. The church building has been a landmark to people entering Eagle River since 1965, when work started on the main structure. The park was named after a Dena'ina chief from Eklutna Village. (Author's collection.)

BIBLIOGRAPHY

Bell, Tom. "Volunteers Hustle to Make Eagle River into Sports Village—Arctic Winter Games." *Anchorage Daily News*, March 3, 1996.

Bragg, Beth. "Ceremonial Start Cut Short—Iditarod: Saturday's Leg of Race Will End in Anchorage Instead of Eagle River." *Anchorage Daily News*, March 1, 2001.

Capps, S.R. "The Turnagain-Knik Region." In *Mineral Resources of Alaska, Report on Progress of Investigations, 1915*. Washington, DC: Government Printing Office, 1916.

Cochrane, Marjorie, and Lee Jordan. *Between Two Rivers: The Growth of Chugiak–Eagle River*. Chugiak, AK: Chugiak–Eagle River Historical Society, 1997.

Community Directory for the Greater Chugiak Area. Chugiak Ladies Club, 1972.

Curran, Hugh. "Bridging Eagle River Briggs Family Helped Little Town Grow, Prosper." *Anchorage Daily News*, October 12, 1992.

Erickson, Jim. "Dick Rapp: From Minnesota Farm to Midtown Anchorage Offices Entrepreneur Finds Fortune in Alaska Land Speculation." *Anchorage Daily News*, December 15, 1985.

Hinman, Mike. "Eagle River Walmart on Track—Big Box Retailer Expected to be Ready by Spring 2000." *Anchorage Daily News*, March 18, 1999.

Kari, James M., James A. Fall, Shem Pete, and Mike Alex. *Shem Pete's Alaska: The Territory of the Upper Cook Inlet Dena'ina*. Fairbanks: University of Alaska, 2003.

McCulloch, David S., and Manuel G. Bonilla. *Effects of the Earthquake of March 27, 1964, on the Alaska Railroad*. Washington, DC: Government Printing Office, 1970.

McKinney, Debbie. "Eagle River: 20 Minutes from Anchorage Is a Plush New Theater, Plus Skating, Hiking, Eating, and More." *Anchorage Daily News*, January 28, 1986.

Medred, Craig. "The Unnatural." *Anchorage Daily News*, November 7, 1999.

Mendenhall, Walter C. "A Reconnaissance from Resurrection Bay to the Tanana River, Alaska, in 1898." In *20th Annual Report of the United States Geological Survey, 1898–1899*. Washington, DC: Government Printing Office, 1900.

Obituary of Glenn Briggs. *Anchorage Daily News*, May 12, 1990.

Obituary of Melva Pippel. *Anchorage Daily News*, July 19, 1989.

Visit us at
arcadiapublishing.com

....